Contents

ANCIENT EGYPT

The Land of Ancient Egypt

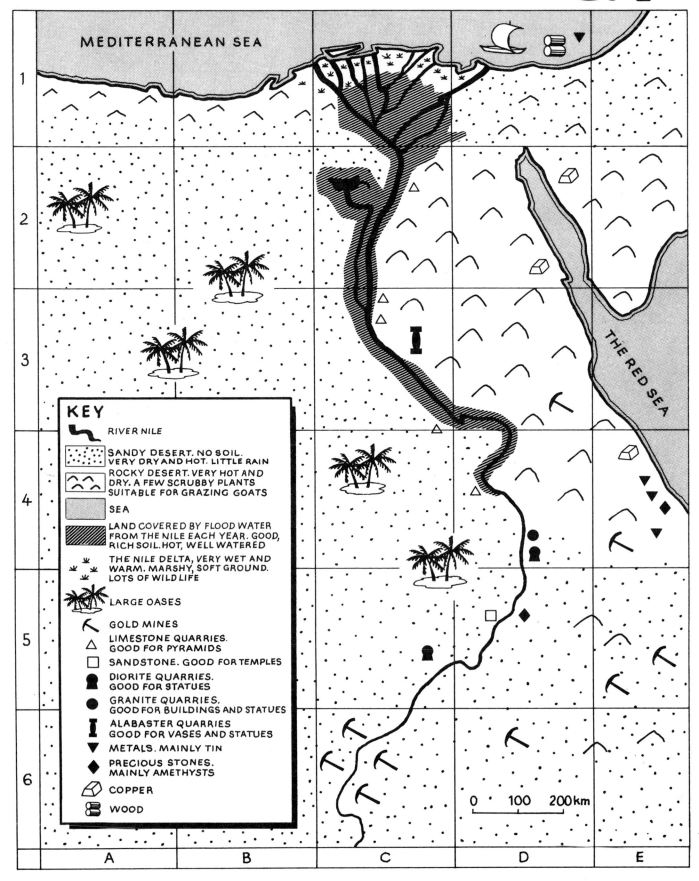

MEDITERRANEAN SEA

THE RED SEA

KEY

~~~ RIVER NILE

SANDY DESERT. NO SOIL. VERY DRY AND HOT. LITTLE RAIN

ROCKY DESERT. VERY HOT AND DRY. A FEW SCRUBBY PLANTS SUITABLE FOR GRAZING GOATS

SEA

LAND COVERED BY FLOOD WATER FROM THE NILE EACH YEAR. GOOD, RICH SOIL. HOT, WELL WATERED

THE NILE DELTA, VERY WET AND WARM. MARSHY, SOFT GROUND. LOTS OF WILD LIFE

LARGE OASES

GOLD MINES

LIMESTONE QUARRIES. GOOD FOR PYRAMIDS

SANDSTONE. GOOD FOR TEMPLES

DIORITE QUARRIES. GOOD FOR STATUES

GRANITE QUARRIES. GOOD FOR BUILDINGS AND STATUES

ALABASTER QUARRIES GOOD FOR VASES AND STATUES

METALS. MAINLY TIN

PRECIOUS STONES. MAINLY AMETHYSTS

COPPER

WOOD

0   100   200km

A   B   C   D   E

The Ancient World

Chris Jordan
Queen Elizabeth's School and Community College, Crediton

Tim Wood
Broadoak School, Weston-super-Mare

Illustrations by
Clyde Pearson

John Murray

HISTORY IN ACTION Chris Jordan and Tim Wood

Already published
England in the Middle Ages

In preparation
Old World and New World

Acknowledgements

The authors and publishers are grateful to Terry Fiehn, Head of the History Department at Parliament Hill School, London, and to Richard Woff, Lecturer in Classics, University of London Institute of Education, for their advice and help.

Illustrations
BBC Hulton Picture Library, 17 (left), 57 (foot); the British Museum, 8 (top, centre and foot), 19, 20, 22 (left), 23, 42, 43; British Tourist Authority, 55 (right); Committee of the Egypt Exploration Society, 21 (foot); Department of the Environment (Crown Copyright reserved), 55; Equinox, 11, 12–13, 15 (top); Grosvenor Museum, Chester, 52; Historic Buildings and Monuments Commission, 53; Michael Holford Library, 17 (lower right); the Mansell Collection, 16, 17 (upper right), 22 (foot), 35, 37, 38 and cover, 39, 48, 51, 57 (top) and cover, 58 (top and foot), 60, 62, 63; Ministry of Culture, Greece, 42 (foot); National Museum of Victoria, 10; Seaphot Ltd, 32; Spectrum Colour Library, 18 and cover; Hirmer Verlag, 9; Roger Wood/Cairo Museum, 22 (right).

Sources for quoted passages
p. 16: quoted in *Social Life in Ancient Egypt*, W.M.F. Petrie (Constable).

pp. 18, 22: *The Histories*, Herodotus (Penguin Modern Classics).

p. 42: quoted in *Athenian Democracy*, Robin Barrow (Macmillan).

p. 43: Table 1 and quotation from *Through Greek Eyes*, Roger Nichols and Kenneth McLeish (Cambridge University Press).

p. 49: *The Twelve Caesars*, Suetonius (Penguin Modern Classics).

p. 50: *Germania*, Tacitus (Penguin Modern Classics).

First published 1986
by John Murray (Publishers) Ltd
50 Albemarle Street, London W1X 4BD

Designed and typeset by DP Press, Sevenoaks, Kent
Printed in Great Britain by Martin's of Berwick

British Library Cataloguing in Publication Data

Jordan, Chris
  The ancient world.—Students' ed.—(History in action)
  1. History, Ancient
  I. Title II. Wood, Tim III. Series
  930 D59

ISBN 0–7195–3954–4

Jordan, Chris
  The ancient world.—Teachers' ed.—(History in action)
  1. History, Ancient
  I. Title II. Wood, Tim III. Series
  930 D59

ISBN 0–7195–4094–1

1 Copy or trace the map. Use colours to show the different types of land found in Ancient Egypt.

2 Copy the table below and complete it by writing in the reference numbers and letters for the squares where each item is found (A1, B2 etc.).

3 See if you can find 4 products mined or dug out of the earth by the Ancient Egyptians. Write their names in your book.

4 Describe the condition of the soil found in C1 and D4.

5 What form of transport was used to bring wood to the land of Egypt?

6 Which 3 squares on the map (A1, B1 etc) would be most suitable for human settlement? Why?

7 Write down 4 ways in which the river Nile was useful to the Egyptians.

RAW MATERIAL	USE	LOCATION
Grain (emmer, barley)	Bread, flour	
Water	Agriculture, drinking	
Mud	Bricks, pottery	
Sand	Bricks, glass, pottery, glaze, abrasive	
Stone	Building, statues, coffins, drinking vessels	
Water reed (papyrus)	Paper, boats, ropes, sandals	
Palm trees	Roofing, boats, oil, dates	
Desert scrub	Grazing for goats	

Flooding of the Nile

Each year the river Nile would flood between July and October. This was known as the 'Inundation'. The water spilt over the banks of the river and soaked the land. The water carried rich soil. When the floods went down, a strip of fertile land was left on the banks.

The Egyptians learnt to trap this water with specially dug basins. It was then let out into channels to water the fields. This good farming land made Egypt rich and powerful. The flood was so important to the Egyptians that they named one of their seasons 'Inundation'.

● The picture shows the Ancient Egyptians using 3 things which they had plenty of (water, mud and sun) to make something useful. Using the picture to help you, describe what everyone is doing. Try to get the right order of events, and do not forget to mention the person sitting down on the right of the picture.

Crafts in Ancient Egypt

Left, spinners at work. Plant fibre, such as flax, was stretched and spun into a long thread using a spindle (**1**). Men and women would spin the thread

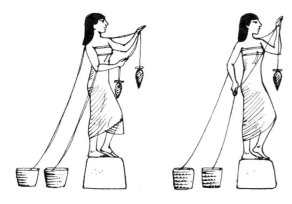

The picture below shows the kind of clothes and hairstyles worn by rich Egyptians around 1500 BC. Both men and women wore long, loose white tunics. Men and women wore their hair in the same style — often a wig. They also wore richly decorated metal jewellery around their necks and wrists.

The People

The first Egyptian settlers built houses along the banks of the river Nile around 4500 BC. They were hunters and farmers looking for good land and water. Gradually they formed into larger groups until there were 2 kingdoms, Upper and Lower Egypt. These were united into one kingdom in about 3100 BC. As farming, trade and industry developed the kingdom became more powerful. Larger cities were built on the banks of the river.

Metal-workers melting bronze. The metal is heated in a furnace (**1**). This is kept hot by the foot bellows (**2**), which blows in air to keep the fire going. The liquid metal is finally poured into moulds (**3**) and left to harden. The mould is then removed

Carpenters at work, making furniture. Notice the tools they are using. (**1**) is a sawing post, used to grip wood while it is being cut. (**2**) is an axe, used to split planks of wood. (**3**) is a drill, used to make holes in a chair frame so that the woven seat can be fitted in

The Crafts

The Egyptians we̶ all
sorts of things. afts
from reeds, p̶ llery
from gold, s̶ ecious
stones. The̶ n small
houses and̶ arnt how
to use co̶ 2 metals
which co̶ ng weapons
and t̶ t how to
write, calculations
(math̶ y made some of
the̶ certainly helped
th̶ r huge monuments

se pages are based on
Egyptian tombs dating
and 1300 BC.

Fashion table' for 2 Egyptians
BC. Draw or write about the
both men and women:

hairstyle   clothes
shoes   jewellery
make-up

2 Picture search. Find each of the following objects on this page. Draw the object in your book and write a sentence saying what it was used for.

kiln   bellows   drill   spindle
potter's wheel

Potters at work, making storage jars and other pottery objects. Clay is trodden in a large pit (**1**), then worked into shape on a potter's wheel (**2**). The pot is then baked and fired in a brick oven, called a kiln (**3**)

Egyptian Farming

Land

Land was very valuable in Egypt. The large amount of food the Egyptians produced was the key to their power. Only the land near the river Nile was good enough for farming. The rest, apart from a few big oases in the western desert, was too dry. Much time and care was taken marking out plots of land. If farmers lost a small amount of land, they could lose much of their wealth.

Ploughing

Water

Water is essential for plant growth. Without regular supplies of water, plants just wither in the heat. Land that is too dry has to be irrigated. This means putting large amounts of water onto the land.

Reaping

Irrigation

The Nile rose by one metre in the summer and flooded out over its banks. The water covered the land for about 60 days. After this time the water began to go down. The fields were divided up by means of dykes and canals into a series of basins. The water was trapped in these for about 40 days before being run off.

Threshing

Farming

The ground was prepared by ploughing. The seed was scattered by hand. Animals like sheep and goats were used to tread the seed into the ground.

When the grain was ripe it was harvested. Only the heads of the grain were cut off. The stalks were left to turn into straw. The grain was then separated from the husks by threshing. This was done by cattle treading the grain out. The farmers then winnowed the grain. They scooped up the grain and threw it into the air. The wind blew away the dust and chaff. The grain was then stored in granaries.

Winnowing and carrying grain to the granary

Crops

Apart from grain like emmer (used for making bread) and barley (used for making beer) the Egyptians grew many other crops. Some of these were lentils, onions, garlic, lettuce and dates. Food was sweetened with honey. Meat was a luxury, but the Egyptians had pigs and goats as well as cattle. Animals were most often found in the swampy Delta.

The Egyptians also ate pigeon, ducks and geese. They grew grapes in the oases and the Delta, and made wine, sometimes from pomegranates and dates. Flax was one of the most important crops. It provided clothes,

ropes and sails for boats. Papyrus was used to make paper and boats, which were rather like rafts.

1 What animals are being used for ploughing?

2 Describe or draw 2 farming tools being used by the Egyptians.

3 Reaping could be boring. What is the man in the left of the reaping picture doing to make this work more fun for the farmers?

4 Draw your own strip cartoon to show the different stages of farming in Ancient Egypt.

A tomb painting, showing scenes of farming in the after-world (see page 14)

The Civil Service and Writing

Egypt was a large area. The ruler, the Pharaoh, could not be everywhere at once. Thousands of servants were needed to check that everything was being organised.

The Land

Servants had to measure and map the land. All Egyptians had to pay taxes to the Pharaoh — usually animals, grain or other farm produce. These taxes had to be counted. Canals and drainage ditches had to be kept in good condition.

The People

It was important to know who people were and what jobs they did. In order to defend the rich land of Egypt, the Pharaoh needed an army. Thousands of workers were needed to build the great monuments and temples.

All this took a good deal of organising. Thousands of the Pharaoh's servants were responsible for this. One of the most important of the Pharaoh's servants was the Southern Vizier. He was responsible for the whole of southern Egypt.

Keeping Records

1 Draw up an account sheet to send to the Pharaoh, listing the taxes collected by the Southern Vizier. Your teacher will suggest how you can do this. You are not allowed to use modern letters (A, B, C etc.), or modern numbers (1, 2, 3 etc.) These are the tax items:

14 bags of gold	24 pottery dishes
10 oxen	2,000 sacks of grain
4 goats	573 sacks of beans
6 gold bracelets	

2 Describe 2 difficulties you had making the list.

3 Why was it important to the Pharaoh that very accurate records were kept?

4 Why did the geography of Egypt make it particularly difficult to rule?

Writing

As the kingdom grew more powerful, keeping records became more complicated. Gradually the Egyptians developed writing and counting to make this easier.

At first they used pictograms or hieroglyphs. This is picture writing, using a small picture for each word. Simple messages can be sent in this way. You can try it for yourself.

But now try to write hieroglyphs for 'green' or 'yesterday'. You will see that this is much more difficult.

Slowly the Egyptians' method of writing changed. They kept hieroglyphics for carving on stone. But they also began to use pictures to stand for certain sounds.

For example — the hieroglyph for stool is □ but it also came to stand for the sound of the letter P.

This is not a message in pictograms about birds, lions, feathers and hands, but a word written in sound signs. It spells out 'Cleopatra'. Sound signs (phonograms) are more useful for writing complicated words.

You can make up your own alphabet and write messages to each other. The only problem is that you will find it is very slow.

The Egyptians found this method of writing slow as well. When scribes wrote on papyrus (see below) they used a brush-like pen. This made the signs more rounded. The words were simpler and quicker to write. This form of writing is called hieratic script. You can compare hieroglyphs and hieratic script by looking at these pieces of writing. Exactly the same words are written in both scripts.

Write out some of the signs in both scripts.

Paper

Papyrus, a tough water plant, was used to make baskets, rope and sandals. But its most important use was for making paper. The pith of the reed was cut into thin slices and laid in 2 layers. It was then beaten together and dried to make paper. Ink was made from vegetable gum and soot. Pens were made from thin rushes.

Information for the civil servants was written down by scribes. One Egyptian advised his son, 'Learn to be a scribe, for this will be of greater advantage to you than all other trades.' Can you think why he gave this advice?

A papyrus or water reed

5 Four methods of passing on information are shown in these pictures. The table shows some important jobs which have to be done by civil servants in one Egyptian district. Copy and complete the table (yours will be bigger) by writing in which method you would use for each job.

Sign language

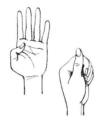

Done with the hands

Knotted strings

These were hung on walls

Hieroglyphs

Usually found on stone tablets or painted on walls

Hieratic script

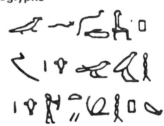

Usually found on papyrus sheets

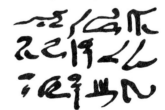

JOB	METHOD USED	REASON
To record all farmers' names		
To write the life history of the Pharaoh		
To count cattle for taxes		
To tell foreign slaves where to work		
To send orders to the army		

The Egyptian Army

1　　　　**2**　　　　**3**　　　　**4**　　　　**5**

The Egyptian Army was a large, very powerful force. It was used to protect the land of Egypt against enemies such as the Nubians and Hittites.

There were 20,000 soldiers in the army at the time of Ramesses II (1292–1225 BC). Most of the men were foot-soldiers. They were trained and skilled in marching and fighting. They wore linen clothes and were protected by long shields made of rawhide. Their main weapons were axes, swords and spears. Weapons were made first of copper but later of bronze. Many foot-soldiers also carried bows.

The army was expected to fight in pitched battles, to patrol the frontiers or to surround enemy strongholds.

Perhaps the best fighters in the army were the chariot soldiers. Fast, light war chariots each carried 2 soldiers. One was the charioteer who drove the horses. The other was armed with a spear, a shield and a powerful bow made of wood, horn and sinew. These could fire accurately up to a distance of 400 metres and were copied from the Hyksos tribe who had moved into the Delta in 1700 BC. The Pharaoh rode in a war chariot when he led his army into battle.

The war chariot made the Egyptian Army very powerful. It was used to break up enemy formations. Chariots were driven straight at groups of enemy soldiers who were lined up on open ground, with the archers firing their bows. When the enemy soldiers ran away the chariots would chase them.

1 Identify by number the soldier or soldiers who carry each of the following weapons:
- (a) bow
- (b) quiver
- (c) club or mace
- (d) spear
- (e) battle-axe
- (f) curved sword or scimitar
- (g) throwing stick

2 Which of these weapons do you think might have developed from Egyptian farming tools?

3 Which weapons would also be used for hunting animals?

4 What can you find out about Egyptian armour from these pictures?

5 Look at the picture of the Battle of Qadesh.
- (a) Draw a chariot without horses.
- (b) What is the difference between the chariots at the bottom of the picture and those described in the text? Why are they different?

Ramesses II at the Battle of Qadesh

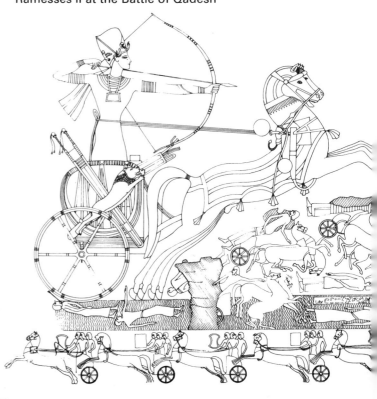

Ramesses III leads the Egyptian Army in a battle against the Sea People

6 **7** **8**

6 From the list below choose 4 sentences which you think best describe the chariot. Write them underneath your drawing.

(a) The war chariot was fast and easy to drive.
(b) The war chariot could carry 5 or 6 men.
(c) The war chariot was also used to carry heavy equipment for the army like corn and tents.
(d) The war chariot was very fast with light wheels and body.
(e) The war chariot carried 1 or 2 soldiers.
(f) The war chariot was a slow and heavy vehicle.
(g) The war chariot was pulled by 2 horses.
(h) War chariots were very quiet when several travelled together.
(i) War chariots were made mainly of wood and leather.

● Look carefully at the picture above.

7 Describe the weapons being used in this battle.

8 Which important part of the Egyptian Army could not be used in this battle? Why not?

9 Which figure is Ramesses? Why do you think so?

10 Who do you think won the battle? Give your reasons.

11 Why was it important for the Pharaoh to lead the army?

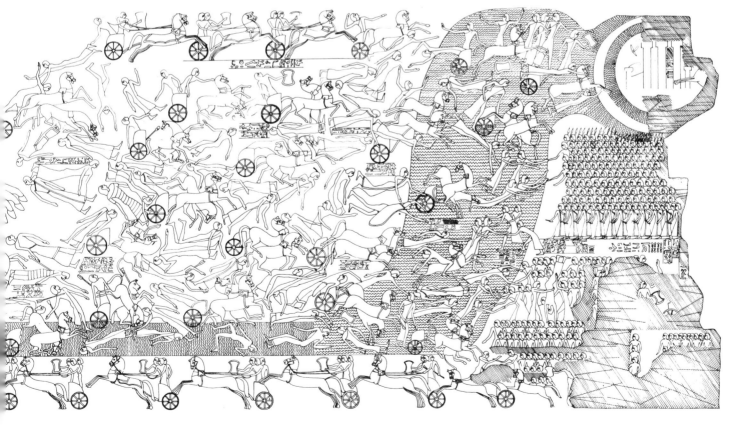

Egyptian Religion

The Egyptians had many deities (gods and goddesses). Local deities and new deities were brought into the religion from time to time. Sometimes one particular god or goddess became popular in an area.

Egyptians were usually very tolerant about religion. They rarely punished people who believed in different religions. They adopted some foreign gods and goddesses.

Re the Sun God

Re was one of the most powerful gods. Sometimes he is shown in his boat. At other times he is shown with a hawk's head and the sun's disc above his head. Other pictures show him as a beetle. (In Egypt there is a curious beetle called the dung beetle. It rolls a small ball of dung along with its back legs — rather like the sun moving through the sky.) Re ruled the sky and decided who should live for ever. The sun could never die.

1 Copy and complete the passage below by putting these words in the correct spaces. Use the information about Re to help you.

> heat crops summer
> deity light
> Nile temples

Like many ancient peoples, the Egyptians looked up to the sun as the most important object in the universe. They turned the sun into a . . . . called Re. The sun was needed to provide . . . . which made the . . . . grow. It also provided . . . . , which allowed them to work. The Egyptians made great use of the daylight hours, especially in the . . . . Great . . . . were built at Heliopolis, an important city on the river . . . . , so that people could worship Re.

The tomb picture on page 15 shows the Egyptians' idea of what happens to the sun at night. The sun disappears at night and reappears every morning. We know why, but the Egyptians explained it like this. Re travelled across the sky in his boat. As it sailed through the night he was in great danger, so he had other gods and goddesses to protect him. The boat was pulled by jackals. The great snake Apopis attacked the boat but the god Seth defended Re. When the sun boat reappeared in the morning the world was happy. Birds sang and baboons screeched. (You can hear the dawn chorus greeting Re to this day.)

Some deities

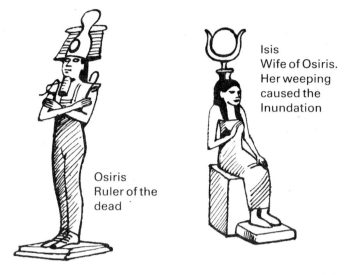

Osiris
Ruler of the dead

Isis
Wife of Osiris.
Her weeping
caused the
Inundation

Horus
The falcon-headed
sky-god of
Upper Egypt

Seth
God of deserts,
storms and war

Thoth
God of writing
and counting

Hathor
Goddess of women,
the sky and trees

The Legend of Osiris

Two of the most popular deities in Egypt were Isis and Osiris. This is one version of their story told by the Greek writer, Plutarch, in the second century AD.

Osiris came to earth as a man and became King of Egypt. He was wise and strong, and under his rule Egypt grew rich and powerful. He made new laws to help the poor and weak and he fought against crime and evil. His wicked brother, Seth, tried many times to get rid of Osiris, but he failed.

One day, Seth found a large magic box which once closed could never be opened. He had it changed to look like a coffin and dared Osiris to lie in it. Osiris got in, and Seth slammed the lid shut. He threw the coffin into the river Nile. It sank, and Osiris was drowned.

However, Osiris' wife, Isis, was a powerful goddess. She used magic to find Osiris' body. She collected spells to bring him back to life. But Isis' magic could only work if the body was whole and perfect, so Seth cut it into 14 parts, and hid them all over Egypt.

Seth thought he had won, but Isis patiently searched for all the parts of the body. She bound them together in linen bandages. Then Osiris was brought back to life. Though he could not return to earth, Osiris became Lord of the Underworld. Here he judged the souls of Egyptians who died.

Isis and Osiris had a son, Horus, who took revenge on Seth. Horus defeated him in battle and killed him. Horus then became King of Egypt.

This legend was very important to the Egyptians. They thought a dead Pharaoh was one with Osiris. The new Pharaoh was thought to be one with Horus. The Egyptians believed in a life after death in Osiris' kingdom.

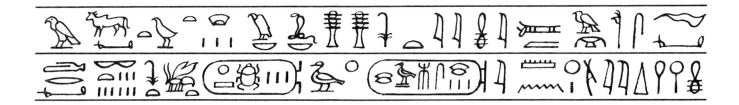

The hieroglyphics above show the full title of the Pharaoh Tuthmosis IV. Roughly translated it reads:

'Horus; mighty bull, perfect, of glorious appearances; lasting ruler like the sun god; strong of arm; conqueror of enemies; King; son of Re; Tuthmosis, mighty, loved by the sun, giver of life like Re.'

2 Draw a picture of any scene from the story of Osiris to be painted in an Egyptian temple.

3 Imagine that Seth was not killed. Make up a new story about the fight between Seth and Osiris.

4 What disasters might happen to the Egyptians for which they might blame the god Seth?

The Pharaoh

This statue comes from the tomb of the Pharaoh Menkaure. The Pharaoh was the ruler of Egypt who had to be obeyed without question.

The word Pharaoh means 'Great House', after the palace where the Pharaohs lived. The Pharaohs said they were directly related to Re, the sun god. They always chose names which showed they were gods.

They made laws and led the army. They also built great temples and monuments. Very powerful Pharaohs built massive tombs for themselves.

The Pharaohs lived in great pomp and ceremony. Priests went with them at all times. They had to make sacrifices to the gods and take part in prayers.

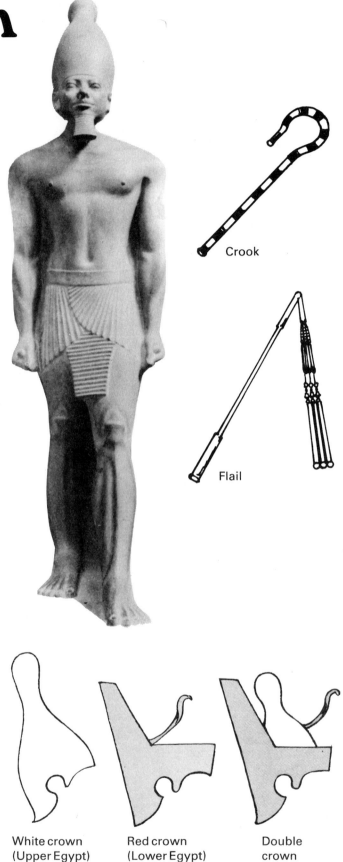

Crook

Flail

'Every hour was definitely set aside for various duties. . . not for pleasure. On rising in the morning the first thing was to read the messages which had arrived, and this probably involved dictating the replies. Then came the ceremonial purification and putting on the robes and badges of office. Then came the sacrifice.

Before this the high priest with the King and people standing around him prayed for the health of the King, recited the praises of the King and then put a curse on all mistakes that had been made, putting the blame on the ministers.

After the sacrifice, the King inspected the entrails. . . he then finished the sacrifice. . . with offerings of wine and oil. Then came the sermon when the priests read the laws and historical passages suitable for the time.

The food of the King is said to have been plain and limited to preserve his health and through this the health of the country.'

White crown (Upper Egypt)   Red crown (Lower Egypt)   Double crown

The Crown

The Pharaoh's crown was 2 crowns in one. The tall white head-dress was the crown of Upper Egypt; the short red head-dress was the crown of Lower Egypt. On the front of the double crown was a cobra. Pharaohs usually wore a false beard and carried a crook and a flail.

1 Why did the Pharaoh wear a double crown?

2 What do you think the crook and flail represented?

3 Explain the last paragraph in the document.

4 Draw and colour the double crown of Egypt.

16

Queen Hatshepsut (1503–1482 BC)

She was the widow of Tuthmosis II. She ruled instead of her stepson, Tuthmosis III. She refused to give up the throne even when he was 18.

She avoided wars and instead concentrated on building up trade. She sent a number of ships to the Land of Perfumes (Punt). This opened up an important trade route for Egypt.

She had some temples and monuments built, but most were pulled down or defaced by Tuthmosis when he became Pharaoh.

Tutankhamun (1361–1352 BC)

He was still a child when he came to the throne. He died when he was only 17 or 18. Very little is known about what he did. There is no record of any wars, but we do know that he had a number of temples rebuilt.

His tomb was discovered in 1922. His possessions and many valuable treasures were found with his mummy. This is the only royal tomb that has been found intact.

Ramesses II (1292–1225 BC)

He was a great soldier who made Egypt more powerful by war and conquest. He fought a long war against the Hittite Empire. At the battle of Qadesh in 1285 BC, he claimed he fought single-handed against the whole Hittite Army and won. It is certainly true that he led and inspired the army.

He signed a peace treaty with the Hittites and married a Hittite princess. This made Egypt safe. Then he built the largest and most impressive monuments and temples in Egypt.

He ruled for over 60 years. He married many times and was the father of over 100 children.

■ ■

1 Say which of the pieces of evidence labelled A, B and C belongs to which of the 3 Pharaohs. Explain why you chose the ones you did.

2 Pick 3 words or phrases from the description of Ramesses which show he was a powerful ruler.

3 Why was it useful to the Pharaoh to be thought of as a god?

4 What might be some of the disadvantages of being the Pharaoh?

5 Why was Tutankhamun soon forgotten?

6 Find out more about the discovery of Tutankhamun's tomb. What is the importance of this Pharaoh to modern historians?

7 Design a picture to be painted on each of these Pharaohs' tombs.

Evidence A

Evidence B

Evidence C

The Pyramids

This picture shows the Great Pyramid (right) which was built by the Pharaoh Cheops. Its bases are 230 metres long. It is over 140 metres high. It is made of 2,300,000 blocks of building stone, each weighing at least 2½ tonnes. Good quality limestone and granite were used to line the walls and give the pyramid a smooth face. It is estimated that 10,000 people worked for 20 years to build it.

The pyramid was built as a magnificent tomb to hold the Pharaoh's body after his death. To make sure that he would go to the after-world it was built on the west bank of the Nile, where the sun set. The burial chamber was placed in the centre of the pyramid, at the end of a narrow tunnel. The Pharaoh's belongings and treasures were buried with him to make sure his after-life was comfortable. The shape of the pyramid is probably meant to represent the sun's rays as they shine down.

Here is a report on the building of the pyramid by a Greek writer, Herodotus:

Cheops came to the throne and plunged into all manner of wickedness. He closed the temples and forced the Egyptians to work in his service. Some were required to drag blocks of stone down to the Nile from quarries. . . others received the blocks after they were sent in boats across the river. . . It took 10 years to make the causeway [ramp] for moving the stones. It is built of polished stone and is covered with carvings of animals.

The pyramid itself was built in steps. They raised the remaining stones by means of machines formed of short wooden planks.

The blocks of stone were carried by boat across the Nile

When the pyramid was finished the ramps were removed. As they came down, the workers covered the outside with fine polished limestone slabs

The heavy stones were dragged up ramps into position. The Egyptians used sledges and rollers to move them

1 Look carefully at the pictures showing the building of the pyramid. Put them in the right order, and then trace or copy them into your book as a strip cartoon, to show how the pyramid was built.

2 Write a report to the Pharaoh on the progress of the building of the pyramid. Mention any problems and suggest what action should be taken to solve them.

3 How is your account of building the pyramid different from that of Herodotus?

4 How much did the pyramid weigh?

5 Why were these things important tools in building the pyramids?
  copper chisel   sledge   rope   boats   jewels

6 Look carefully at the map and the table below. Copy them carefully into your book. You must decide on the best site for the Great Pyramid. Complete the table by writing ✓ or ✗ to answer the questions. The site with the most ticks will be the best one. Remember that it is easier to float a heavily laden boat down towards the sea with the current.

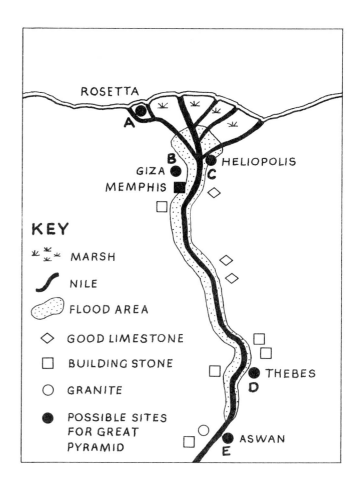

KEY

🌿🌿 MARSH

〰️ NILE

⬭ FLOOD AREA

◇ GOOD LIMESTONE

▢ BUILDING STONE

○ GRANITE

● POSSIBLE SITES FOR GREAT PYRAMID

	SITE A	SITE B	SITE C	SITE D	SITE E
Is it near building stone?					
Is it near Memphis (the capital city)?					
Is it on the west bank of the Nile?					
Is it safe from floods?					
Can granite and good limestone be taken there easily? (You can use boats)					
Has it good foundations? (Not marshy)					

The huge limestone slabs were cut and shaped with copper chisels with jewels in them. Sometimes wooden wedges were put into the rock and then made wet. This made them swell and split the stone

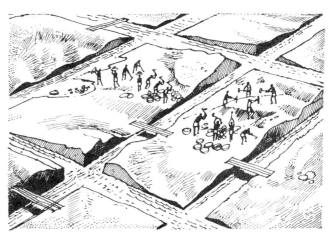

The ground where the pyramid was to be built was cleared and levelled using channels filled with water. They used the stars to line up the sides

Embalmer

See Teachers' Notes page 4

The Egyptians believed they would continue to live after death. The spirit (or *Ba*) would leave the body as a large bird and fly to the after-world. This could only happen if the body was in perfect condition.

To keep the dead in perfect condition, the Egyptians preserved them by turning them into mummies. This stopped them from decaying. This may have begun because the Egyptians noticed that bodies buried in hot desert sand became dry very fast. The drying preserved the body.

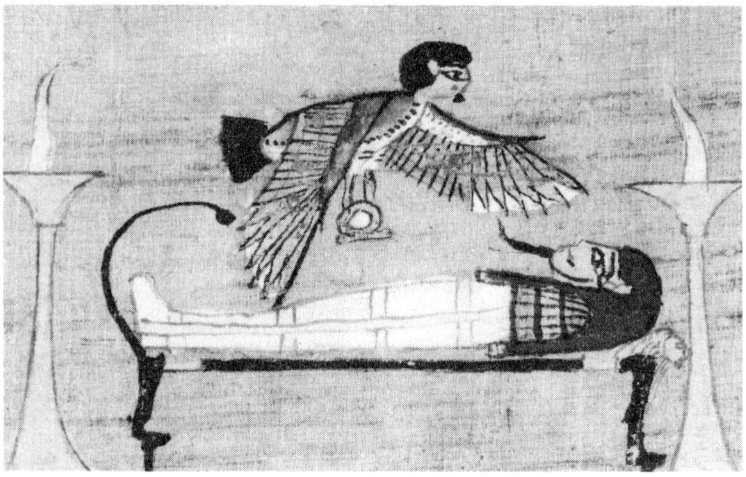

The Ba leaves the body

As burials became more complicated, with larger tombs and coffins, bodies no longer came into contact with hot sand. So they had to be artificially preserved. The people who did this were called embalmers.

- You have been given a job as an embalmer in Memphis around 1500 BC. You must prepare a mummy from a dead body by completing 6 steps from the table opposite.

1 Place a small counter (e.g. a coin) on any of the boxes (a, b, c) on Stage 1. You move down the page from stage to stage, selecting only one box on each line. At each stage, note down the box you choose.

2 You will need a special item to enter some boxes (marked ✻). Before you start, choose 3 items from the list below. If you do not have the right item for a box you must choose another box in that row.

3 Write down the 3 items you choose and what each of them does. Think carefully about the effect of each item on the dead body. Will it preserve the body or make it decay faster?

4 When you have finished, show your list to your teacher, who will work out your score. If you score more than 10 points you have been a successful embalmer.

A *Chaff and straw*
Old bits of straw, linen, salt, herbs and dust. Swept from the floor of the sacred temple at Memphis.

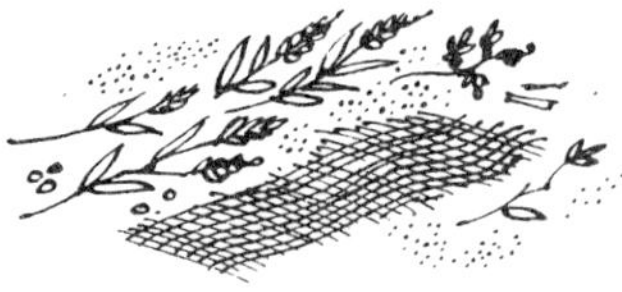

B *Knife*
A very sharp-bladed knife used to cut the body open to remove the brain, liver and other important organs.

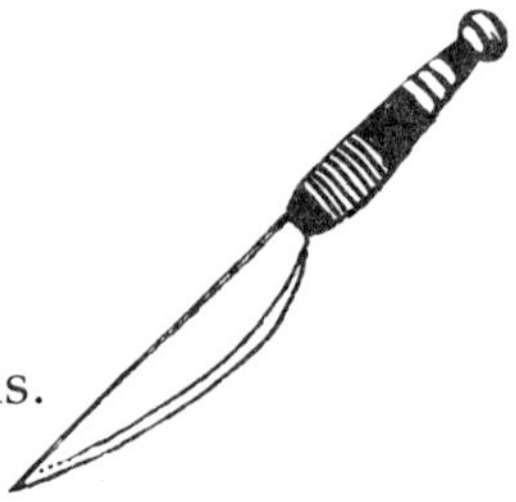

C *Nile water*
Nile water blessed by the priests. It could be used to wash the body.

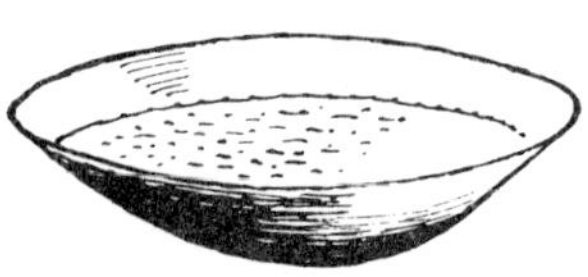

D *Natron*
A special form of dry salt. Supposed to have magical powers. It is a dry, white powder found in the desert. It dries things completely.

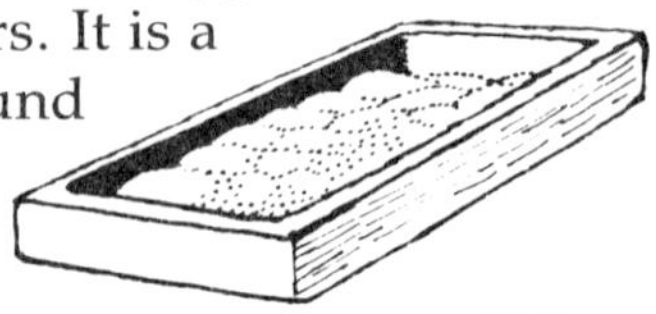

E *Cedar oil*
A sweet-smelling oil made from the leaves of the cedar tree. It will slowly wear away flesh and tissue.

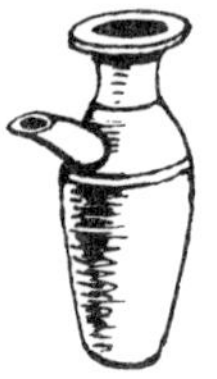

F *Lotus flowers*
These are large, fleshy flowers which grow in the river Nile. They are thought to be the holiest of all plants, given directly by the sun god.

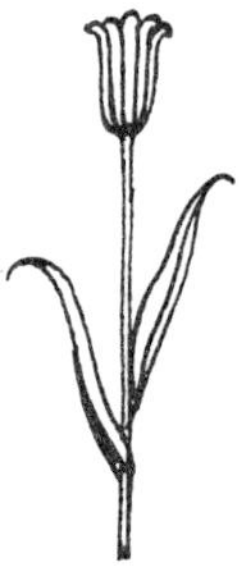

STAGE 1

(a) ✱ Inject body with clear cedar oil

(b) ✱ Take out liver, brain and other organs

(c) Remove eyes, toenails and fingernails

STAGE 2

(a) ✱ Soak body in a bath filled with Nile water

(b) ✱ Soak body in bath filled with cedar oil

(c) ✱ Bury body in natron for 40 days

STAGE 3

(a) ✱ Pad out chest muscles with straw and chaff

(b) Put herb cream on any wounds

(c) Draw picture of the sun on body's chest

STAGE 4

(a) ✱ Cover body with lotus flowers

(b) ✱ Rub cream, oil and perfume, all over the body

(c) Stitch up wounds or cuts

STAGE 5

(a) Wash body in herb water and spices

(b) Cover body in mud from the river Nile

(c) Cover body with thick sticky resin which will dry hard

STAGE 6

(a) Wrap body in fresh linen bandages from head to foot

(b) Put body in a large sack

(c) Tie up body with fresh knotted reeds and ropes

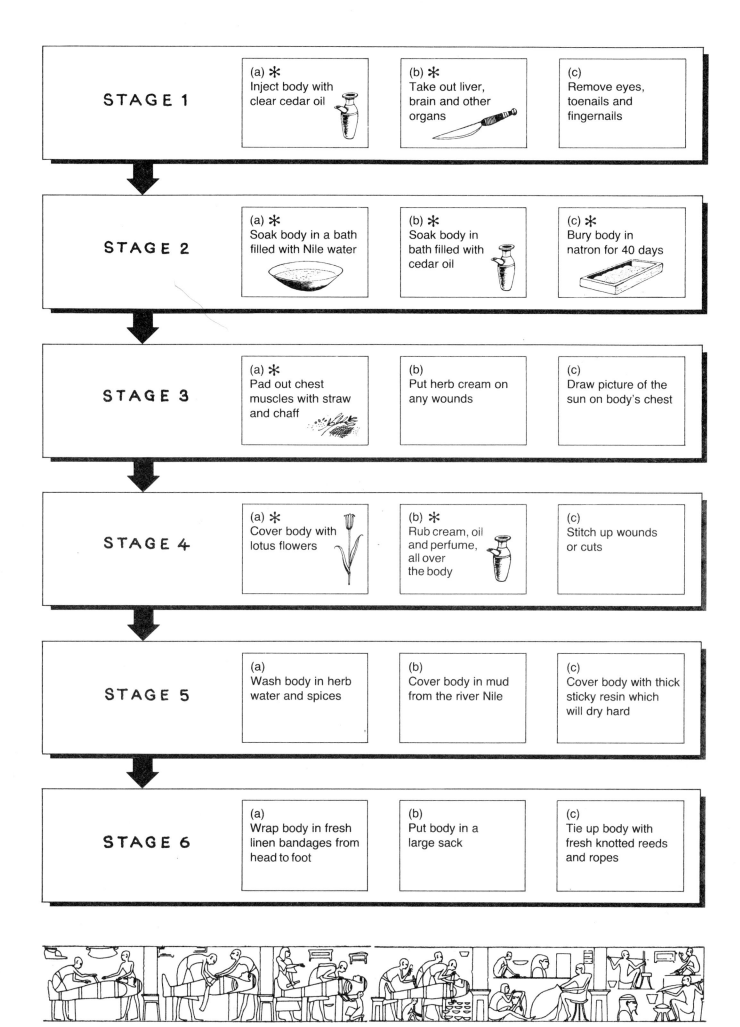

The picture comes from a tomb in Thebes. It shows some of the stages in preparing a mummy

21

Mummies

You should have found out by playing the embalmer game (page 20) that the best way of preserving a dead body is to remove the internal organs and replace them with a mixture containing dry salt or natron. The following pieces of evidence show clearly how and why the Egyptians mummified their dead. Look at them carefully.

What?

A Mummy and mummy case

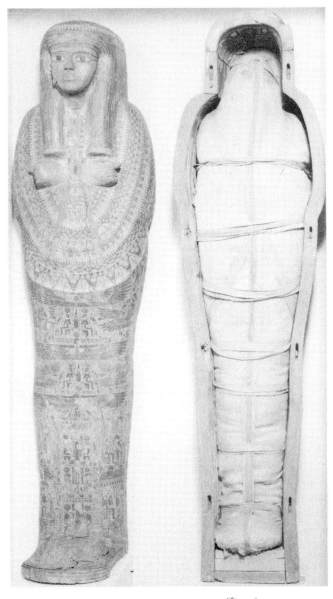

B The organs were stored separately in stone jars (known as canopic jars)

C Head of the mummy of King Ramesses II

How?

D Eyewitness account by Herodotus

Herodotus was a Greek writer who visited Egypt and wrote about his experiences in a book called *The Histories*.

He said that the Egyptians never buried or burnt their dead but paid embalmers to preserve their bodies.

> First they draw the brain through the nostrils with a metal hook. . . next with a sharp Ethiopian stone, they make an incision in the flank and take out the entrails. . . Having done this they cover the body with natron. . . then they wash the corpse and wrap the whole body in fine linen cut into strips, smearing it with gum. . .

E Modern research

In 1975 a research team cut open an Egyptian mummy kept at Manchester University (mummy 1770) and carried out a series of experiments on the body. They found that:
1 The body was still in very good condition (it was over 2,000 years old).
2 The body contained no internal organs and there were signs of a cut in its side.
3 The body had a false leg made of reeds. (The research team thought that the real leg had been bitten off by a crocodile and that this could have been the cause of death.)
4 The body was that of a delicate girl, aged about 13. There was no evidence to show that her parents were rich.
5 Further experiments showed that filling the body of a dead rat with dry salt could keep it fresh for up to 3 months.

F The Hall of Two Truths

Why?

The Egyptians believed in life after death. This life would be similar to life on earth. So they placed the possessions, clothes and furniture of the dead in their tombs for them to use in the after-life. Food and scenes from people's lives were painted on the walls.

The dead spirit would travel through many gates, each one guarded by animal-headed deities. It would reach the Hall of Two Truths to be judged by Osiris, ruler of the dead, and 42 other deities. The spirit would say it had done no wrong in life. This was tested by weighing the spirit's heart against the feather of truth. If the scales balanced the spirit passed into the after-world (Yaru) where it enjoyed all the best things of earthly life. If the scales did not balance, the soul was eaten by a monster called the 'Devourer'.

G A mummy was transported to the tomb by boat. Small models of boats like the one shown here have been found in tombs

1 Study the evidence on these pages. Read the following statements and write down only the ones that are true.
  (a) Mummies could wake up hundreds of years after being buried.
  (b) Only the bodies of rich people were mummified.
  (c) Embalming was an essential part of Egyptian religion.
  (d) Mummies were thieves or murderers who were buried alive.
  (e) The Egyptians believed there was life after death.

2 Write a detailed description of the work of an embalmer. Use the evidence on these pages to help you. You can illustrate it.

3 Does modern research agree or disagree with the evidence given by Herodotus?

4 Make a display of pictures and models of Egyptian life to go in a tomb.

5 Can you think of another reason why the mummy examined in Manchester had a reed leg?

Tomb Robber

See Teachers' Notes page 5

This is a game for 2 or 3 players. One is the Pharaoh's architect, the other(s), a gang of tomb robbers. Your teacher will tell you how to play.

CHAMBER	EXPLANATION	HOW LONG IT DELAYS THE ROBBERS
Pharaoh's tomb	The holy room containing the sarcophagus, mummy and treasure.	2 hours
False tomb	Looks like the Pharaoh's tomb but contains no mummy or treasure.	1 hour
Deep pit	Deep smooth-sided hole. Drains water and delays thieves.	1 hour
Dead end	Passage blocked by a huge stone which must be moved.	3 hours
Secret passage	Like a dead end but there is a hidden door you must find.	2 hours
High door	The passage ends. The door is hidden high up on the wall.	1 hour
Falling stone	A huge stone which crashes down on top of you if you step on the wrong part of the floor. You must move the stone.	3 hours
False passage	A passage which appears to go somewhere but soon ends.	1 hour

Tomb robbers

Your aim is to enter the pyramid and explore it. You want to find the Pharaoh's tomb so you can steal the treasure. Make a suitable token or counter to show your gang moving inside the pyramid.

Robbers' equipment

EQUIPMENT	USE
Long rope with metal hook	Pit, high door.
Ladder	High door.
Metal crowbar	Pharaoh's tomb, false tomb, dead end, secret passage, falling stone.
Torches	All tunnels and chambers are dark. It will be hard to move without torches. Without them you only move at half speed — 1 square per 2 hours.
Water	All the tunnels and chambers are hot. If you take water you can add an extra 5 hours to your time in the pyramid.
Money	To bribe the guards. Toss a coin to find if they take it. If they do you can add 5 hours to your time in the pyramid.

GREAT STAIRCASE

24

26   25

Pharaoh's architect

Your aim is to make the inside of the pyramid a safe place for the Pharaoh's tomb. You do this by putting 8 chambers into the pyramid. You can see these on the top table opposite. You must note down the numbers of the squares where you place the chambers. You can only use each ⚠️ chamber once.

These chambers are designed to trap robbers or delay them long enough for the guards to catch them.

You must announce each chamber as the robber gang enters it. Keep a careful note of the number of hours that pass.

1 Write an imaginative account of your tomb robbery. You can illustrate it.

2 Why was it difficult for architects to design robber-proof tombs?

3 Design your own robber-proof tomb.

4 Explain why you think the Pharaohs gave up building pyramids and instead had secret tombs built in the Valley of the Kings.

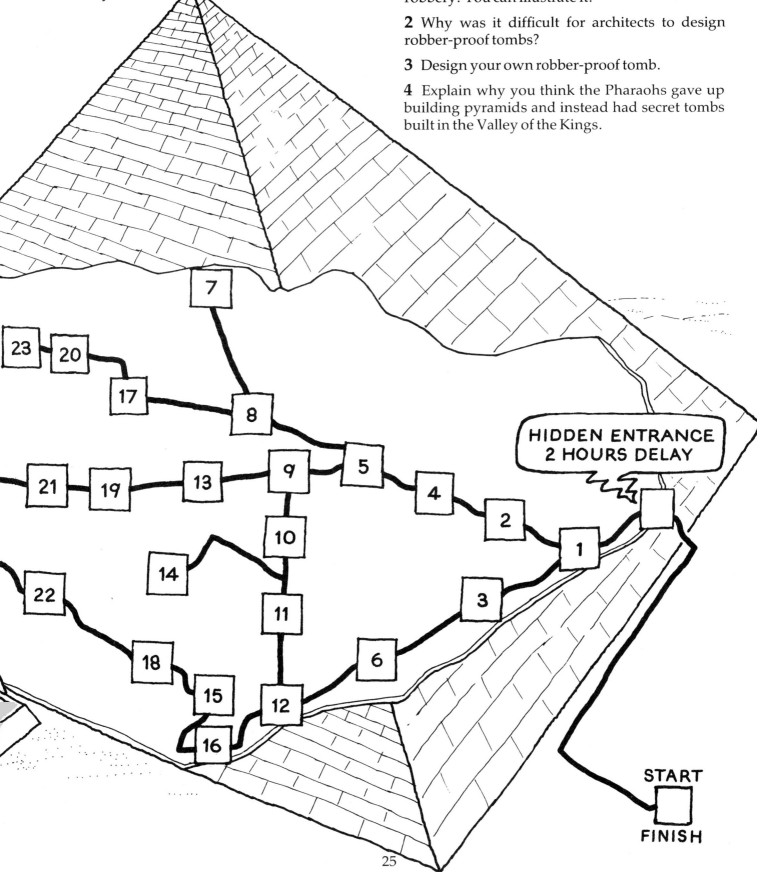

HIDDEN ENTRANCE 2 HOURS DELAY

START

FINISH

25

Excavation at Giza

See Teachers' Notes page 5

This is a detective exercise based on the evidence on these pages. You are going to make a report on the excavation by working through the evidence below and answering the questions given on page 64. (The numbers in brackets in the text refer to the diagram on page 27.)

Background

In about 2070 BC, King Cheops, son of King Snofru, built the first of the great pyramids at Giza. Cheops was a very powerful Pharaoh and this was the largest pyramid ever built. It was over 140 metres high and covered with smooth limestone slabs.

A   *The excavation of the shaft*

In AD 1924, Dr Reisner, an archaeologist, began to excavate the Royal Cemetery at Giza. He dug close to the Great Pyramid (1). He found 3 small pyramids (2), built for Cheops' Queens, and Cheops' mortuary (death) temple (3). He also found an unfinished pyramid with a hidden entrance (4). He was excited by this. It might lead to an undiscovered tomb. He began to investigate.

- Look carefully at the diagram on page 27 and read facts **1** to **13**. Then start your report by answering section A of the questions.

B   *The discovery of the tomb*

At the bottom of the shaft Dr Reisner found a small tomb (see facts **14** to **16**). He carefully cleared the floor. Every piece was marked on a plan, photographed and catalogued. Notes were taken at each stage. These covered 1,600 sheets of paper. It took 326 days to clear the tomb.

- Go on to section B of your report.

C   *Inside the tomb*

Among the objects found in the tomb were:

- A great tent-like canopy 2½ metres high. The beams and posts were encased in gold. It was broken in pieces. An inscription on it suggested that King Snofru had given it to his wife.
- A great bed with golden legs shaped like lions. It was broken in pieces.
- 2 gold-covered armchairs.
- 8 alabaster jars of oil, perfume and make-up.
- A manicure set.
- Several boxes of rings, shut tight — containing chips of alabaster from the sarcophagus.
- A gold drinking cup and 2 gold plates.
- Several gold sheets.

The sarcophagus looked as if it had been forced open.

Dr Reisner reached 3 conclusions:
1 He knew whose body was in the sarcophagus.
2 He was sure the funeral objects had once been in a much larger tomb and had been reburied here.
3 He believed that the building of the tomb and the reburial had been done in a hurry.

- Go on to section C of your report.

D   *The mystery of the tomb*

At last the tomb was cleared. On 3 March 1925 the sarcophagus was opened. It was empty. Why had anyone bothered to go to such great trouble to bury an empty sarcophagus?

- Discuss the evidence with your group. Work out why there was no mummy in the sarcophagus and what had happened to it. The extra evidence in the table opposite will help you. Then go on to section D of your report.

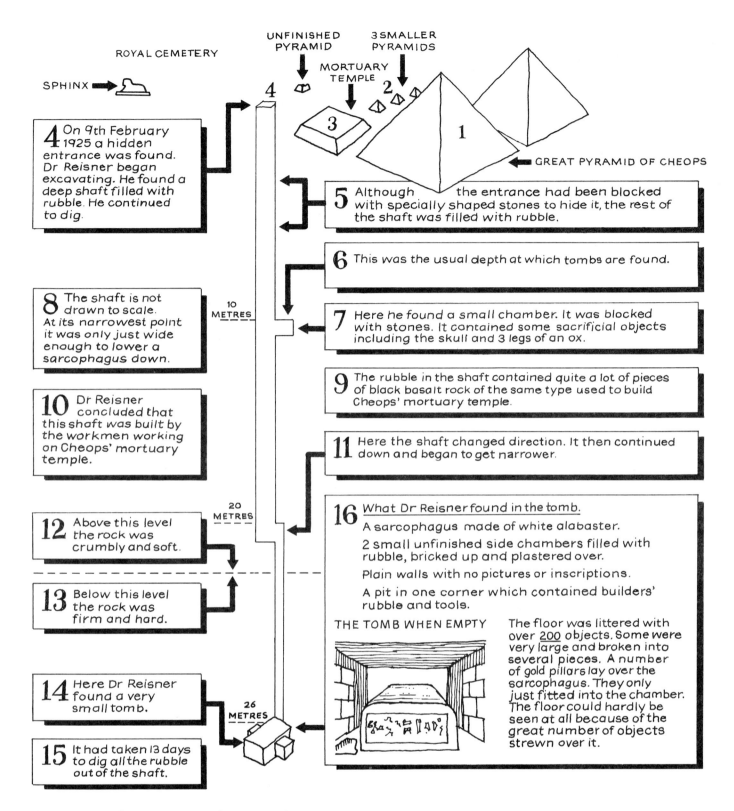

ROYAL CEMETERY

UNFINISHED PYRAMID

3 SMALLER PYRAMIDS

MORTUARY TEMPLE

SPHINX ➡

GREAT PYRAMID OF CHEOPS

4 On 9th February 1925 a hidden entrance was found. Dr Reisner began excavating. He found a deep shaft filled with rubble. He continued to dig.

5 Although the entrance had been blocked with specially shaped stones to hide it, the rest of the shaft was filled with rubble.

6 This was the usual depth at which tombs are found.

8 The shaft is not drawn to scale. At its narrowest point it was only just wide enough to lower a sarcophagus down.

10 METRES

7 Here he found a small chamber. It was blocked with stones. It contained some sacrificial objects including the skull and 3 legs of an ox.

9 The rubble in the shaft contained quite a lot of pieces of black basalt rock of the same type used to build Cheops' mortuary temple.

10 Dr Reisner concluded that this shaft was built by the workmen working on Cheops' mortuary temple.

11 Here the shaft changed direction. It then continued down and began to get narrower.

20 METRES

12 Above this level the rock was crumbly and soft.

13 Below this level the rock was firm and hard.

16 What Dr Reisner found in the tomb.

A sarcophagus made of white alabaster.

2 small unfinished side chambers filled with rubble, bricked up and plastered over.

Plain walls with no pictures or inscriptions.

A pit in one corner which contained builders' rubble and tools.

THE TOMB WHEN EMPTY

The floor was littered with over 200 objects. Some were very large and broken into several pieces. A number of gold pillars lay over the sarcophagus. They only just fitted into the chamber. The floor could hardly be seen at all because of the great number of objects strewn over it.

14 Here Dr Reisner found a very small tomb.

26 METRES

15 It had taken 13 days to dig all the rubble out of the shaft.

Extra information for section D

King Snofru was buried at the Royal Cemetery at Dashur – 12 miles from Giza.	There is a small pyramid near Snofru's pyramid at Dashur where his wife may have been buried. It is empty.	The most valuable jewels and treasure were always put into the bandages round the mummy.
During the building of the pyramid of Cheops, the tombs at Dashur would not have been guarded very well.	Robbers often burnt the dry bandages in order to steal the gold sheets which were wrapped round the mummy.	The official in charge of a Royal Cemetery would lose his life if the Pharaoh discovered that he had actually lost a royal mummy.

The Greek City-States

Greece is a country with many limestone mountain ranges. These mountains are cold, dry and have little soil. The plains (flat land) between the mountains generally have fertile soil and good water supplies, and so are better places for people to settle.

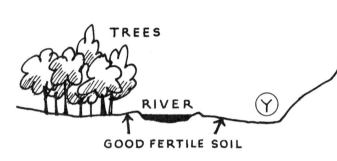

1 Copy this diagram into your book. Give 3 reasons why Y is a better site for a settlement than X.

2 Imagine that 500 people move onto plain Y. Choose from the list opposite the type of settlement most suitable for most people.

A *One large city*. Will be easy to organise and defend. Houses can be built around a central fort. Will take time and co-operation.

B *Many small villages*. Easily built but will use a lot of land. Each village will need to be defended.

C *Tents*. Quickly put up and easy to move. Easily wrecked in bad weather. No defence if attacked.

Greek City-States

In about 700 BC, there was no single ruler of Greece. Instead, the country was divided into a number of city-states which traded with one another, and sometimes fought one another. The centre of each city-state (*Polis*) was one town or city. For example, Athens was the city that controlled the area known as Attica. The Polis made the laws and ruled all the people inside its territory. There were hardly any fixed boundaries between city-states. Plato, the Greek writer, said the Greek cities were like frogs round a pond (see the map on page 30).

Most cities and city-states were fairly small, sometimes with only a few thousand people and a territory of between 10 and 15 km². Athens, however, is thought to have contained about 200,000 people, and the area of Attica was 800 km². As one city became large or powerful it might try to take over more of the countryside around it, and armies would be sent to attack rival cities. But no city-state was strong enough to control the whole of Greece.

The city-states began to expand by setting up *colonies* on islands or parts of the coast around the Mediterranean Sea (look at the lower map opposite). By the fifth century BC, small groups of states began to join together to defend themselves. They would form a league of alliance, such as the Delian League (478 BC). Philip II of Macedon became the first ruler of the whole of Greece after he defeated the Athenians at Chaeronea in 338 BC.

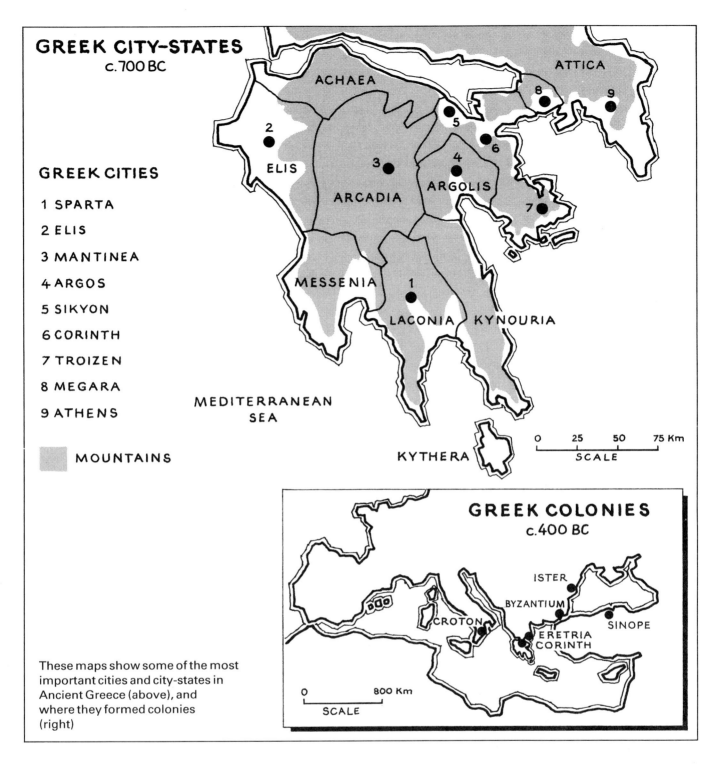

GREEK CITY-STATES
c.700 BC

ACHAEA

ATTICA

8

9

2

5

ELIS

6

GREEK CITIES

3

4

1 SPARTA

ARCADIA

ARGOLIS

2 ELIS

3 MANTINEA

7

4 ARGOS

5 SIKYON

MESSENIA

1

6 CORINTH

7 TROIZEN

LACONIA   KYNOURIA

8 MEGARA

9 ATHENS

MEDITERRANEAN
SEA

MOUNTAINS

0   25   50   75 Km

SCALE

KYTHERA

GREEK COLONIES
c.400 BC

ISTER

BYZANTIUM

CROTON

SINOPE

ERETRIA
CORINTH

These maps show some of the most
important cities and city-states in
Ancient Greece (above), and
where they formed colonies
(right)

0   800 Km

SCALE

Sparta quickly became a very powerful city because it had a large, well-trained army. This army was sent to attack other cities, and to take over their land. Sparta gained control of the states of Messenia, Kynouria and Kythera in this way. Other cities decided that it was better to come to an agreement with Sparta, so they became allies of Sparta. This happened to Arcadia, Elis, Megara, Troizen, Sikyon and Corinth. The remaining city-states (Attica, Argolis and Achaea) refused to join with Sparta and looked for land elsewhere to make themselves more powerful.

1 Copy the map into your book, and colour it. Use one colour to show states controlled by Sparta, another colour to show allies of Sparta, and a third colour to show independent states.

2 Name the city-states around each of these cities:

(a) Sparta
(b) Athens
(c) Argos
(d) Mantinea

3 What is a colony?

4 Explain how the map of Ancient Greece changed between 700 and 400 BC.

29

Greek Trade 1

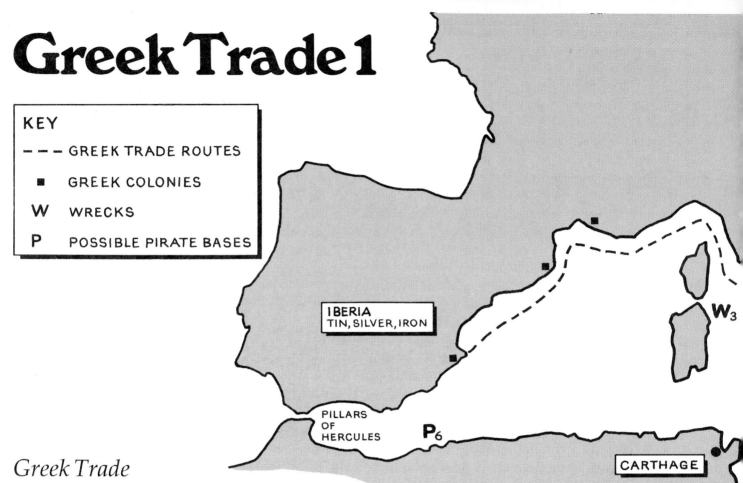

KEY
- --- GREEK TRADE ROUTES
- ■ GREEK COLONIES
- W WRECKS
- P POSSIBLE PIRATE BASES

IBERIA
TIN, SILVER, IRON

PILLARS
OF
HERCULES

P_6

W_3

CARTHAGE

Greek Trade

The sea was very important to the citizens of Attica and the other city-states. It was far easier to travel by ship than in carts or on horseback, and large ships were built to travel around the coastline and out to the islands in the Aegean Sea. When large cities like Athens found they could not produce enough food for all their citizens, they began to trade for wheat. Ships would leave the Athenian port of Piraeus loaded with olive oil and silver and exchange it for wheat at another port. Soon Greek ships began to visit Crete, Sicily and Egypt in order to trade. Athens quickly became the leading trading city in Greece: Athenian craftsmen produced fine pottery which could be exchanged for wine, iron and slaves. Then the Athenian traders began to use money. They would buy goods with silver coins and sell them in foreign ports.

The ships could be wrecked by a sudden storm, attacked by pirates, or destroyed by other trading ships, but generally these trading voyages were very successful, and the ship owner could make a lot of money. Trade routes were established across the Mediterranean Sea; most ships kept to the coastline, but a longer journey could result in a bigger profit.

A Greek Trading Voyage

Many citizens and slaves were involved in trade. Some made goods for sale, while others made up the crew of a merchant ship. Any rich man could trade. He would need money to buy a cargo (he might borrow it at 12% interest from a moneylender). Then he would set sail, and return home months later with a new cargo to sell in the markets in Athens.

- The main trade routes and cargoes are shown on the map above. A typical voyage to Thrace could be shown by this flow-chart.

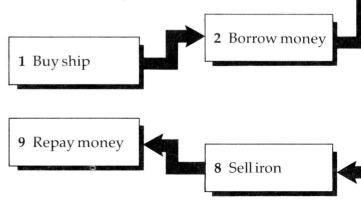

1 Buy ship → 2 Borrow money

9 Repay money ← 8 Sell iron

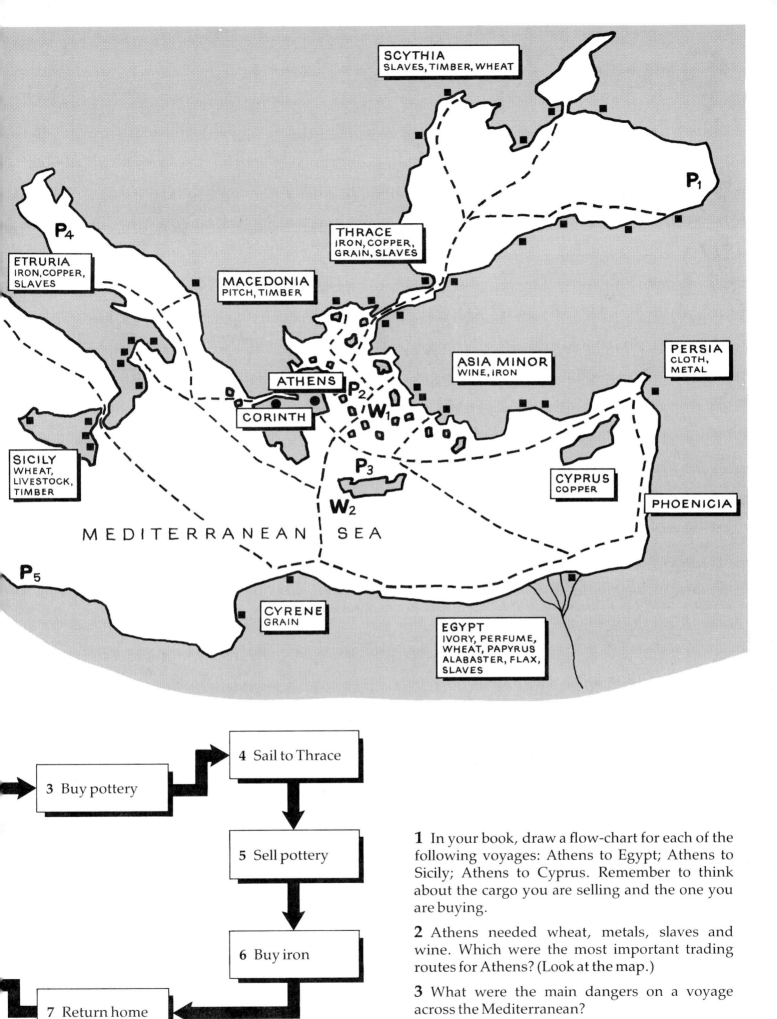

SCYTHIA
SLAVES, TIMBER, WHEAT

P₁

THRACE
IRON, COPPER,
GRAIN, SLAVES

P₄

ETRURIA
IRON, COPPER,
SLAVES

MACEDONIA
PITCH, TIMBER

PERSIA
CLOTH,
METAL

ASIA MINOR
WINE, IRON

ATHENS

P₂

CORINTH

W₁

SICILY
WHEAT,
LIVESTOCK,
TIMBER

P₃

W₂

CYPRUS
COPPER

PHOENICIA

M E D I T E R R A N E A N   S E A

P₅

CYRENE
GRAIN

EGYPT
IVORY, PERFUME,
WHEAT, PAPYRUS
ALABASTER, FLAX,
SLAVES

4 Sail to Thrace

3 Buy pottery

5 Sell pottery

6 Buy iron

7 Return home

1 In your book, draw a flow-chart for each of the following voyages: Athens to Egypt; Athens to Sicily; Athens to Cyprus. Remember to think about the cargo you are selling and the one you are buying.

2 Athens needed wheat, metals, slaves and wine. Which were the most important trading routes for Athens? (Look at the map.)

3 What were the main dangers on a voyage across the Mediterranean?

4 Why did people want to trade?

31

Greek Trade 2

See Teachers' Notes page 6

Ships and Cargoes

These are 2 of the main types of Athenian ship.

Merchant ship

Size: A fairly short ship (about 24 metres). Suitable for cargo. Lightly built. Some had room for 20 oarsmen, others could take up to 50.

Speed: This ship had 1 mast and a sail which could be raised to catch the wind. The crew had to row as well. Quite slow and steady when loaded, with an average speed of about 3 mph. When unloaded, it could travel much faster.

Use: Cargoes were carried in the large hold. Grain, iron or slaves were packed in as tightly as possible.
The largest Greek merchant ship we know about was one of 1,800 tonnes which carried grain across the Mediterranean. An empty merchant ship was fast enough to be used by pirates.

1 Imagine you are the owner of a merchant ship. Write 2 or 3 sentences about a trireme, pointing out the advantages it has over your ship, and say why it could be dangerous.

Wrecks

2 Imagine that modern archaeologists have discovered wrecks of Greek ships at the points marked W1, W2 and W3 on the map on page 31. Use your knowledge of Greek trade and the information below to explain:
  (a) Where you think the ship was from
  (b) Where you think it was going
  (c) Why it sank.

W1: This was a trireme with 170 oars. It had a large hole below the waterline and carried no cargo.

W2: This was a small ship with 20 oars. It had a large hold containing 300 jars of olive oil. It was found in deep water. The timbers were widely scattered and parts of the ship have still not been found.

W3: This was a large ship with 100 oars. It was found near a reef, with several smashed planks below the waterline. The hold was full of skeletons and chains.

Modern divers find a Greek jar (amphora)

32

The Ancient World

TEACHERS' NOTES

■■■

Contents

■■■

The History in Action series

History in Action consists of three books which are designed to provide a practical core for a lower school history course. Each book reflects the themes and periods most commonly chosen by teachers for the first three years in secondary schools.

The series should be seen as a skills-based, practical framework around which teachers can fit their own materials. The books consist mainly of self-contained double-page spreads which will provide a lively reconstruction of selected periods of history. They give a sample of the lifestyles and problems of people in particular periods, and in particular environments.

Aims

For the pupil: the books are designed to make history come alive by involving pupils with the problems and decisions of the past. Many of the exercises require pupils to work in groups, and encourage discussion, analysis and problem solving. We have tried to provide participation for children of all abilities. The exercises and activities are meant to encourage the development of a network of personal attainments and co-operative skills. These include reading a passage thoroughly; understanding maps and diagrams; looking carefully at pictures; examining and assessing evidence; balancing fact and opinions; sorting out fact from fiction; co-operating with others; stating opinions; answering questions; decision-making; dramatic reconstruction; and developing an understanding of people and situations.

For the teacher: the books are designed to provide usable, classroom-based teaching material. The teachers' notes offer advice on classroom management, and also many suggestions for extension work. These include reference to a variety of approaches and guidance on how and where to find extra material and sources. The exercises are graded to provide activities for pupils of different abilities.

Contents

The books contain a wide variety of exercises and activities. Some of these will be familiar, others less so.

Text. Each double-page spread contains pictures, documents and questions. The text links these together and provides the background for and a specific introduction to the exercises. Teachers may like to provide their own text or notes to expand the theme.

Documentary material. Many pages contain extracts from original sources. Some of these have been adapted to make them easier to read. Although many questions and exercises are provided, teachers may wish to use the documents as a basis for further work.

Pictures. Many pictures are taken from original sources. Others have been adapted to make them simpler. Every picture forms an integral part of the exercise it accompanies and teachers may like to use them as the basis for further work.

Group work. Some exercises are designated as group work, but most are in fact suitable for this.

They are a good opportunity for mixed ability groupings. Groups can be provided with extra books and materials from departmental resources.

Roleplay. Some simple roleplays are included. Senior pupils or teachers can take these roles. It is most important that they read their briefings in advance. Simple costumes and props can be used. Actors should be encouraged to enliven their roles and perform, rather than simply read.

A list of questions should be discussed and prepared by the class in advance. Teachers may like to devise extra characters and write suitable roles.

There are many advantages in using roleplay. It is a particularly useful way of encouraging questioning. Written work can be empathetic or analytical.

Games. All the games included are based on authentic documentary sources. It is vital for teachers to play the games themselves in advance. The simple board games virtually run themselves. More complex games will need more careful preparation and teachers should monitor the progress of pupils carefully.

The purpose of board games is firstly to provide a great deal of information in a concentrated and palatable form, and, secondly to individualise and enliven a particular problem. All pupils should be encouraged to participate. The game forms a framework for empathetic extension work. Teachers may like to provide further information and sources.

Further work. Individual research may lead to project work on major topics (e.g. Greek city-states, life in the Roman Empire). Pupils will approach this with a greater degree of understanding and involvement.

Model making, pictures and display are all encouraged and are often suggested in the text. Drama work can also be developed.

There are suggestions for obtaining slides and illustrative material on pp. T2–3.

■■■

The Ancient World

Contents
This book is divided into 3 sections:

1 Ancient Egypt (pp.4–27). This section concentrates on the daily lives of the people of Ancient Egypt. It examines agriculture, the army and government and looks at major advances in technology. The later exercises use the evidence of excavations and digs (burials and pyramids). Practical work is stressed throughout the exercises. The main topics are the Nile, farming and trade, crafts, developments in writing, the Egyptian Army, the Pharaohs, religious beliefs, the excavations at Giza.

2 Ancient Greece (pp.28–45). This section attempts to show the effects of the main social, political and economic pressures in the Greek city-states, concentrating on classical Athens and Sparta. It includes material from a number of original sources in a series of exercises and games. The main topics are the city-states, trade and shipping, colonies, Sparta, democracy and slavery. There is a major exercise on the Peloponnesian War.

3 Ancient Rome (pp.46–63). This section examines Rome and the Roman Empire at the height of its power, looking especially at the rule of the Emperor Claudius and the Roman military machine. The exercises are intended to give impressions of major aspects of Roman rule, rather than a detailed history of the Empire. The main topics are the size of the Empire, the powers and problems of the Emperor, the Legions, the lives of the ordinary soldiers, the campaigns in Britain and Europe and life in the city of Rome.

Original source material
Major original sources which may be useful include Herodotus: *The Histories*; Thucydides: *The History of the Peloponnesian War*; Suetonius: *Lives of the Twelve Caesars*; Pliny: *Letters*. These are all available in Penguin translations.

Peter Conolly's *The Roman Army* (Macdonald 1975) includes many extracts from contemporary writers, as well as many useful illustrations based on original sources. Short extracts, pictures and other documentary evidence can be found in many of the books listed on p. T3.

Filmstrips and slides
Slide packs can be compiled using simple slide mounts. Sources for filmstrips and slides are:
1 The usual commercial sources, e.g. Longman, Visual Publications, EAV.
2 Local museum services may have slide packs, especially on the Roman Empire.
3 LEAs usually have a resource service which often operates through school libraries.
4 Make your own. A useful article on this by Nigel Morgan appeared in *Teaching History* October 1981 ('Photography and the History Teacher').

Books and other teaching materials

Books

A full booklist follows. County Library Services are very helpful. With advance notice they are often able to assemble a set of books on a given theme. This is especially useful for project work on topics, such as the pyramids.

The books listed here should be useful if you wish to prepare extra classroom material.

The Secrets of Tutankhamun, L. Cottrell (Evans 1965)
The Warrior Pharaohs, P.H. Newby (Faber & Faber)
Egypt of the Pharaohs, A. Gardiner (Oxford 1964)
Atlas of Ancient Egypt, J. Baines and J. Malek (Phaidon 1980)
The Year of Salamis, P. Green (Weidenfeld & Nicholson 1970)
Ancient Spartans, J.T. Hooker (Dent 1980)
Discovering the Greeks, P. Kenneth Corsar *et al.* (Edward Arnold 1977)
Sparta, R. Barrow (George Allen & Unwin 1975)
History of Rome, M. Grant (Weidenfeld & Nicholson 1978)
The Roman Army, P. Connolly (Macdonald 1975)
Life and Leisure in Ancient Rome, J.P.V.D. Balsdon (Bodley Head 1969)
Atlas of the Roman World, T. Cornell and J. Matthews (Phaidon 1982)

Shire Publications Ltd have produced useful guides on Roman topics, using primary evidence. Topics include Roman forts in Britain, pottery in Roman Britain, Roman crafts and industries, Roman roads. Further details can be obtained from Shire Publications, Cromwell House, Church Street, Princes Risborough, Aylesbury, Bucks.

Edward Arnold's *History Action Pack* (C. Jordan and T. Wood) includes games on the Roman Empire and Slavery.

Museum visits

Museums usually provide a comprehensive service for teachers in their local areas. This may include arranging talks and visits, and supplying catalogues or other materials. Very often the schools' loan service will include working models of Roman or Greek machines or houses. Some of the more important museums that include displays on Roman town life are the Museum of London; Corinium Museum, Cirencester; Jewry Wall Museum, Leicester; Verulamium Museum, St Albans; and Bath Museum. Military sites that can be visited include Piercebridge Roman Fort, Durham; Burgh Castle, Norfolk; Richborough Castle, Kent; and Caer Gybi, Holyhead, Gwynedd. The Ancient World is a good theme for a day trip. The new Greek and Roman displays at the British Museum are informative and well planned for school parties. The schools' radio programme *Curse of the Pharaoh* (from *History Mysteries* for 11–14 year-olds) would also be useful.

Notes on using the book

Always read through the exercises carefully in advance. Try to picture them in action and anticipate problems with individual groups. Work out answers to questions before the lessons.

Read through any introductory text with the class, asking questions to ensure that they have understood, and add your own exposition and ideas wherever you want to. Two or three carefully chosen slides shown in conjunction with an exercise will often prove more useful than a filmstrip, and will be a great aid to understanding.

Some ideas and hints for running and extending the exercises follow.

The Land of Ancient Egypt (p.4). Ex.6: the most suitable squares for human habitation are C1, C2, C3. Note that the west bank was more extensively cultivated than the east bank.

The people in the picture are making bricks by mixing earth and water (plus sand), pouring the mixture into moulds and letting it dry in the sun. The person on the right is an overseer.

Follow-up work might include drawing or studying a map showing settlements in Ancient Egypt, and further exercises on the red land and black land.

The Crafts of Ancient Egypt (p.6). Ex.1: both men and women wear wigs, jewellery (bracelet, neck collar) eye make-up. Woman has a perfume block on her head. The fashion table should start like this:

	Men	Women
Hairstyle	Black wig	Black wig

(Pupils may wish to write full sentences or draw large pictures.)

Egyptian Farming (p.8). Ex.3: the person on the left of the picture is a flute player. Strip cartoons should show the inundation and irrigation.

The Civil Service and Writing (p.10).
Keeping records. Pupils must use pictures instead of letters and numbers. They should find three major problems in using pictograms.
1 Drawing a reasonable likeness of a difficult object (e.g. ox, goat).
2 Showing the difference between similar objects (e.g. sacks of grain being different from sacks of beans).
3 Indicating quantities. Fairly simple if they can

just repeat the drawing the necessary number of times, but difficult for large numbers (e.g. 2,000).

This should encourage them to devise:
1 Simplified pictures which can be easily repeated.
2 Some system of counting using pictures (e.g. hands for 10s, or special symbols for 100s, 1,000s etc.).

Writing. This theme is continued here with the introduction of the need to communicate ideas, which are much more difficult to convey with pictures, and will almost certainly lead to an increase in the number of pictures used.

The object of Ex.5 is to get pupils thinking about the best methods for different situations. Counting could be done with string; instructing foreign slaves will have to be done with signs; orders to the army should be portable, e.g. on papyrus, and are complicated enough to warrant hieratic script. The other tasks could be done by hieroglyphs or hieratic script.

The Egyptian Army (p.12). The Sea Peoples were raiders from the north. They seem to have been made up of several different groups and may have eventually been absorbed by the Philistines. The drawing is from a relief showing a naval battle in the Delta in 1182 BC, when Ramesses III (1198–1167 BC) defeated the Sea Peoples. Chariots were used in an earlier land battle against the Sea Peoples, but obviously could not be used in this battle, which was fought on water.

Egyptian Religion (p.14). The ball rolled by the dung beetle is its food (dung) — believed by the Egyptians to be its egg.

Ex.4: Seth might have been blamed for sandstorms and droughts. Possibly the worst disaster which could befall Egypt would be failure of the inundation. There is evidence that this occurred in the reign of Pepy II (2246–2152 BC), leading to a collapse of royal power in the 7th and 8th Dynasties (2150–2134 BC). Unified royal power was restored by Mentuhotep (2061–2010 BC).

The Pyramids (p.18). Ex.1: foundations could be levelled in the following way. A grid of trenches was dug and filled with water. Workers then cleared out all the rock between the trenches until the whole area was level. The trenches could then be filled in with rubble.

Ex.2: try to encourage pupils to produce imaginative reports about the building of the pyramid, looking carefully at the illustrations and thinking about the work involved.

Ex.3: the main 'mistakes' in Herodotus'

account are the assumption that somehow the Egyptians were enslaved to build the pyramids, and that 'wooden' machines were used. There is no evidence for either assumption. For excellent descriptions and diagrams of pyramid building see Bains and Malek, *Atlas of Ancient Egypt*, pp. 138–139. It seems most likely that pyramids were built using ramps and sledges, though there is still a lot of guesswork about the actual process.

Ex.6: the best site should be B (Giza).

Embalmer (p.20). The idea of 'Embalmer' is to show the stages of preservation. Pupils may not be successful in choosing the right route, but they will be encouraged to think about the process.

The 3 items they should choose are chaff and straw; incision knife; and natron. Teachers can allow pupils to do the exercise without much comment. In the follow-up discussion emphasise that the point of mummification was to preserve the body and arrest the process of decomposition. Lotus flowers and cedar oil would not have had the right effect (although cedar oil would have made the process more pleasant). Nile water was thought to have magical properties, but the body would have had to be dried off carefully.

Separate storage of internal organs would obviously help. The whole process took about 70 days. The most important part was dehydrating the body and covering it in natron.

Ex.4: *Scoring*

Stage	Box a	Box b	Box c
1	0	2	0
2	0	0	3
3	1	1	0
4	0	1	1
5	1	0	2
6	2	0	0

The stages were:
1 Evisceration and removal of the brain.
2 Sterilisation of the body with natron (40 days).
3 Padding out the body cavities with resin and dry materials.
4 Anointing the body and covering it with resin.
5 Bandaging and decoration with charms etc.

Mummies (p.22). These exercises can be related back to previous work on religion and 'Embalmer'. Slides of tombs can be shown to illustrate funerary objects; illustrations from the *Book of the Dead* are especially helpful in explaining theories on life after death. Good accounts of mummification and the philosophy of it are given in *Death in Ancient Egypt*. A similar mummy investigation was recently carried out at Bristol Museum.

Tomb Robber (p.24). This is a board game. Pupils play in pairs or threes. One player is the Pharaoh's architect, the other(s) a gang of tomb robbers. Play the game yourself to develop your own simple explanation.

The board represents the inside of a pyramid, with passages linking 26 numbered chambers. The architect aims to design a robber-proof tomb, while the robber tries to steal the Pharaoh's treasure.

One hazard is already on the board – the secret entrance. This delays entry into the tomb for 2 hours; but like all the hazards, once passed it ceases to operate. It does not delay robbers escaping from the pyramid. Other hazards are allocated to numbered chambers by the architect. So each game will differ according to where the architect places hazards.

Robbers move along the passages from chamber to chamber. With a torch, it takes 1 hour to get from one chamber to the next. Robbers can only move to a chamber adjacent to the one they are in. They may retrace their steps.

Before the game begins, the architect decides where each of the 8 special chambers listed in the *Chambers* table will appear on the board. Architects may choose any of the numbered chambers. They must not mark the board, but keep a secret note of their choice. (Architects could make counters representing each hazard, to be placed face down on the board before play starts.) While architects place the hazards, robbers choose 4 items of equipment from the *Equipment* table. They write down their choice.

Play

1 Robbers place a suitable token (coin, drawing pin, or they could make their own) on START, and move it from chamber to chamber along any route.
2 Architects note carefully the time taken — remembering that it takes one hour to travel between chambers, even if robbers are retracing their steps.
3 When a robber enters a hazard chamber, the architect says which hazard it is. The robber must have the correct item of equipment to pass (see *Equipment* table), and proves this by showing his or her equipment list to the architect.
4 Without the correct item the robber cannot pass, and must find another route. (NB: the false passage is a dead end, so no equipment will help.)
5 Architects use the *Chambers* table to note the time taken for robbers to pass through special chambers.
6 Robbers must enter the pyramid, find the

treasure and return to start within 30 hours (or more with some items of equipment), or lose the game.

Extra work

1 Once played, the game is simple, and you may like to allow pupils extra games. They should change roles at some stage.
2 Players who fail to find the treasure can re-enter the pyramid and try again. The board should not be altered but robbers can choose 4 new items. This should show clearly why the robbers always had the advantage.
3 Robbers could write imaginative accounts of their robbery. Architects could prepare a piece of work, either defending themselves to the Pharaoh after a successful theft, or explaining the secret of their successful design.
4 This pyramid did not exist. It is made up of features from a number of royal tombs, some of which are not pyramids at all (loosely based on the tombs of Sahure, Cheops, Seti I and Amenemhet III). Pupils could be invited to design their own robber-proof tombs, protecting them with traps and curses.
5 There is scope for extra research into the Valley of the Kings and actual tombs.

Excavation at Giza (p.26). It is suggested that pupils work in small mixed-ability groups. Teachers should lead the pupils through the evidence, asking key questions and getting them to work stage by stage. The pupils then investigate the evidence for themselves and make a report by answering the questions at the back of the book (page 64). (For convenience, page 64 may be duplicated by teachers for use within the school.) Pupils should work through the 4 sections one at a time. Section E contains extra questions which you may wish to use as well.

The story: (A full account can be found in Chapter VI of *Lost Pharaohs*) Reisner concluded that the mummy was Snofru's wife (Hetepheres). He believed that her tomb at Dashur was raided. First the robbers unwrapped the mummy and removed the jewels. Then they set fire to the body. They broke open a number of boxes (the attack on the sarcophagus causing chips of marble to fly into these boxes). At this point they were disturbed. The official at the tombs reported the raid but did not dare to report the loss of the royal mummy. Cheops ordered his workers to stop building his own mortuary temple and to dig a tomb for his mother's body at Giza where it might be guarded better.

The new tomb took longer than anticipated because the rock was so poor. This meant they had to dig much deeper. They were not able to build properly, and had to finish it quickly (hence the lack of decoration and other signs of haste – we can assume that the Pharaoh did not actually climb down to supervise the work himself). The possessions were thrown in hurriedly. The sarcophagus went in without being checked (to the relief of the official). The small pyramid was abandoned in case the secret entrance to the new tomb should be discovered.

Answers to questions (p.64).
A 1 Entrance hidden, shaft blocked.
  2 Upper level of rock soft and crumbly.
  3 Two attempts to hollow out chambers.
  4 Cheops' workmen (basalt chips).
B 1 339 days.
  2 Careful work, need to catalogue.
  3 No decorations, side chambers, rubble, tools, mess.
C 1 Make-up, perfume, manicure.
  2 Snofru's wife (inscription).
  3 Mother.
  4 Shaft narrow: precious objects thrown in.
  5 (*See* C1, C2). Too many objects to fit small space, some broken to get them in. General mess and unfinished state of tomb.
D 1 . . . his mother's tomb had been broken into by robbers.
  2 . . . the royal mummy had been destroyed. . . the Dashur official was afraid of being executed.
  3 . . . to rebury his mother.
  4 . . . to dig a tomb.
  5 . . . soft rock.
  6 . . . more difficult than he had thought, and so was rushed.
E 1 When the robbers broke into the sarcophagus at Dashur.
  2 So that Cheops could keep his eye on it.
  3 To disguise the entrance.
  4 It was taking too long, and they had to get on with Cheops' temple.
  5 Workmen – to get it into the small tomb.
  6 Official at Dashur – loss of mummy remained undiscovered.

Reports can be presented with illustrations.

The Greek City-States (p.28). The map can be used to point out the length of the coastline, and the small space available for settlement.

Greek Trade 1 (p.30). Note that shipowners have to borrow money to buy a cargo; they should choose one that will sell in the ports they visit.

Greek Trade 2 (p.32).
W1: Probably an Athenian warship, destroyed in battle by ramming.
W2: Probably a cargo ship destroyed in a storm after leaving Crete.
W3: Probably a ship carrying slaves from Etruria (Italy); probably rammed by pirates.

Sparta (p.34). This large section of text could be broken down into group work, with groups gathering information on the various sections of Spartan society. Alternatively, teachers might like to use the information to give an illustrated 'tour' of Sparta, explaining the city to the class as to a group of visitors.

Athens and Democracy (p.36). Democracy Exercise. Frustrations and difficulties encountered by the class in the debate should be carefully noted.
First stage: choosing a judge. Your speech might concentrate on your natural advantages – age, education, authority. Keep it short. Count votes by raised hands; no talking. The 10 Strategoi represented the tribes of Athens, and took only military decisions; however one of them might be seen as a judge or leader, such as Pericles who was re-elected Strategos 15 times.
Second stage: Prepare for this by having the class list written out; cut out each name and place them all in a tin. Ask a member of the class to draw out 3 names.
Third stage: This should be carefully limited to 10 minutes. Encourage as much participation as possible, but preferably allow only one speaker at a time. The **president** should choose the speakers. It will be important to discuss all the implications of this exercise once the poster has been completed. All members of the class should take careful notes of what happens during the lessons.

Follow-up discussion should concern not only the poster itself, but also the method of choosing the painters, the way the assembly conducted itself, and why certain people were elected.

Athens (p.38). Ex.2: the speech-writing may need some preparation and help. Teachers might like to suggest a number of points to be covered – buildings, marriages, trade, warfare – and divide the class into groups. Pictures should be encouraged to add to the written work; perhaps a frieze or pot might be designed to show the virtues of Athens.

The Agora (p.40). Ex.1: pupils can use the whole of the section on Ancient Greece as resource material for this exercise.

Slavery in Athens (p.42). Most visual sources show female slaves performing household duties, as opposed to the industrial/farming duties of male slaves described in the text. Ex.4: Plato kept slaves as personal attendants. Nikias used slaves as workers in his silver mine. Ex.3: either Slave A or Slave B would be freed. Assess answers according to quality of reasoning.

Athens and Sparta at War (p.44). Pupils take the part of Athens, at war with Sparta. They make a token and move it round the board, gaining or losing a variable number of points according to the circles they land on. Sparta's score rises by 1 point per move – see *Information*, p.45.

Game procedure
1 Divide the class into groups of 2 or 3 pupils of mixed ability.
2 Let pupils copy the score-card below onto a piece of rough paper.
3 Explain the rules of the game. Note that circles with plus numbers are friendly states which give tribute, soldiers and ships. When pupils land on a 'plus' circle, they add the number to their score-cards. Circles with minus numbers are enemies, allies of Sparta. They fight hard and cost soldiers, ships and supplies. Pupils subtract the minus numbers in the circles they land on from their total strength. (They do not add them to Sparta's score.) Circles marked with an asterisk are risk circles. Pupils must come to you (see below for details) to find out how they score if they land on one of these. Pupils must note their score, and what happens to them, after each move, *before* drawing the next row on their score-cards.

There are several winning routes. The one that most accurately reflects Pericles' policy of collecting as much tribute as possible from the Eastern Empire and trying to set up a western Empire is as follows: D–C–T–S–U–V–W–Y–Z–X–R–O–Q–P–M (on M they decide *not* to attack Syracuse) –N–H–L. Players who follow this sequence will move onto K on move 18, with a score of 21 to Sparta's 20.

Other winning sequences will all require players to avoid the plague which broke out in Athens, also the disastrous expedition to Syracuse. These were the two most important reasons for the defeat of Athens.

Follow-up work. Pupils can write an account of the game they played. They should be asked to include the routes they followed; where tribute was found; what happened in Attica and Athens (D and E); what the results of the expedition to Syracuse were. Teachers might like to go on to study particular aspects of the war with their

---

Risk circles. Information on Risk circles can be presented orally, or you could make a set of cards with the letter of the circle on one side, and the information on the other. Pupils copy the information and the score.

D Plague has broken out in Athens because the people are crowded together in unhealthy conditions. Score −4.

E Plague has broken out in Athens because the people are crowded together in unhealthy conditions. This has now spread to Attica. Score −4.

I Your army is attacked by Spartan patrols. You drive them back but at a terrible cost in casualties. Score −2.

K Sparta. You defeat Sparta if you now have more points than Sparta.

M* You must now decide whether or not to attack Syracuse on the island of Sicily. You know that this is a very rich city. It is also an ally of Sparta, and so your enemy. It could be dangerous to leave the army of Syracuse to attack you from behind. You believe that this army is not very strong and there could be lots of loot to win. When you have decided whether or not to attack Syracuse, report to your teacher who will tell you your score.

O Your allies tell you that they have been attacked by ships from Syracuse, a city on the island of Sicily. Syracuse is one of Sparta's allies. Score 0.

P Your allies tell you that they have fought and destroyed 6 ships from Syracuse. The enemy did not fight well. Much loot was captured from them. Score 0.

Q The weather has become rather stormy. This delays you. Score 0.

T You have attacked the pirate base of Scyros, defeated the pirates and taken much loot. Score 1.

V There has been a revolt on the island of Lesbos. You have defeated the rebels and taken tribute from them. Score 1.

M – The attack on Syracuse. Players who decide to attack Syracuse score −6. Players who decide not to attack Syracuse score 0. NB: An attack on Syracuse counts as part of the move onto M so players do not have to miss a turn, whether they attack or not.

Background information: The Athenians began their siege of Syracuse by trying to build a wall right round the city. They were unable to do this and their fleet was trapped by the Syracusans. The Athenian Army tried to retreat overland, but was cut to pieces by the Syracusans. All were killed or made slaves.

Score-card

Move	Circle	What happened/points gained or lost	Athens total	Sparta total
	D	–	4	2
1				3
2				4
3				5

etc., up to 26 max.

etc.

classes, especially the extent to which the strength of Syracuse was underestimated.

A useful and entertaining extension of this theme is provided by the computer game *Tyrant of Athens* produced for the 16K Spectrum by Lothlorien Games. This has the same basic format as *Kingdoms* although the graphics are not as good.

The Roman Empire (p.46). The game could be played in pairs, or each member of the class can build up his or her own Empire. This exercise works well as homework. Explain the rules carefully, especially no. 5 about movement of Legions. Pupils could make a table like the one below to record the progress of their army and the number of legions at their disposal. Point out to pupils that they have to keep an eye out for narrow passageways between countries, and that mountains can be crossed. The best route is as follows: Rome – Italy (and South Gaul) – Spain – Carthaginian Empire – Egypt – Carthaginian Empire – Spain – Italy and South Gaul – Macedonia – Asia Minor – Macedonia – Gaul – Britain – Gaul – Macedonia – Dacia – here they discover they cannot conquer Germany.

Follow-up work should look at the size of the Empire and the opponents of Rome. The maps in Peter Connolly's *The Roman Army* are very helpful for follow-up work.

Conquering the Empire

Where you are/province conquered	No. of legions
Rome (start)	2
Italy	4
etc.	etc.

The Roman Emperor (p.48). The summary below gives the decisions actually taken by Claudius. Other answers may be justified by members of the class.

The Reign of Claudius. Decision 1 = Action 2. Claudius was not as silly or weak as people imagined. He did not give in easily when the governor of Upper Illyricum led a revolt against him; he used the army to smash the revolt and to arrest the powerful Senators who had supported it. *Decision 2 = Action 4.* He made the Empire even larger, especially by the successful invasion of Britain in AD 43. *Decision 3 = Action 2.* He also sorted out Rome's grain supply by paying for imports and rebuilding the port of Ostia for grain ships. *Decision 4 = Action 1.* His principal advisers were Narcissus, a Greek ex-slave, and Lucius Vitellus, a Roman Senator. There were many plots and conspiracies against Claudius, including one organised by Messalina, his first wife. Messalina and her friends were arrested and executed. Claudius died suddenly in AD 54. Many historians believe that he was murdered by his second wife, Agrippina.

The Legions 2 (p.52). Four legions and 4 legions of auxiliaries gives the most well-balanced force. Catapults can be made on campaign. Elephants will be a lot of trouble. Some food would be taken but the plan was to forage, so as much cavalry as possible should be taken.

Life at the Top (p.58). Try the board game first. The winner should be a pupil who switches ladders rather than staying on one ladder for all 10 moves. Check that each pupil makes only 10 moves.

Life at the Bottom: Slavery (p.60). Ex.6: answers:

Object	Place	Slave
loaf	wheatfield / mill / bakery / shop	field slave / shop slave
glass	aqueduct / fountain	public slave / household slave
jug	silver mine / shop	mine slave / shop slave

Trireme

Size: A very long (35 metres) and narrow ship, powered by 170 oarsmen, sitting in 3 banks.

Speed: The oarsmen were fit, well trained and well paid. They were not slaves. They were kept in time by a flute-player. A trireme could move quite quickly — about 7 mph.

Use: The trireme was a warship. It had a large, solid ram at the prow (front) which often had a metal tip. The trireme attacked merchant ships or other warships. In 330 BC Athens had 492 triremes, a fleet big enough to defeat any other city-state.

Pirates

On the map are 6 possible areas for pirates to set up bases to attack shipping (P1 to P6).

3 Give each site a mark out of 5 for each of the points listed below—5 marks if it is very good, 1 mark if it is very bad and so on.

A   Is it near a trade route, so that the rowers do not have to work too hard?

B   Is it near an area where there are plenty of ships, so that the crew do not have to wait too long for a victim?

C   Is it a good distance from the Athenian Navy? Athenian warships patrol the Aegean Sea. Pirates do not want to meet them.

D   Is it easy to escape and hide after an attack? Pirates want to be near places to hide, like bays or islands.

E   Is it near busy ports? Pirates want to be near busy ports so they can sell their plunder and get new recruits.

POINTS	P1	P2	P3	P4	P5	P6
A						
B						
C						
D						
E						
Total						

4 Write a report to the commander of the Athenian Navy explaining where you think the pirates are based. Explain why the other sites are unlikely to be pirate bases.

5 Write an imaginative account of a pirate attack. You can illustrate it if you like.

33

Sparta

People

Sparta was the only important city in Laconia. In 450 BC, about 8,000 male citizens lived in the city. They were known as **Spartiates**. The land in Laconia was divided into large estates. Only Spartiates could own these. No Spartiate could trade, so land could not be bought or sold. The Spartiates formed themselves into a very powerful army of foot-soldiers (**Hoplites**). Every Spartiate had to pay taxes, live in a military barracks, serve in the army and send his sons to a state school. In return, he had the right to a place in the Citizens' Assembly, which made the laws for the state.

Spartiates spent their time hunting, fighting and training, or on official state duties. Sparta was the only Greek city that used iron coins instead of gold or silver. One writer, Plutarch, said that no teacher or silversmith should bother to visit Laconia, since no one would want their services. The Spartiates were fit and well trained, and the army was famous for its toughness.

The **Outlanders** were free men who lived either in Sparta or in the country. Many were skilled craftsmen, who made weapons and armour for the Hoplites, as well as hard-wearing clothes. They could join the army or the navy, but they could not become citizens. They had no right to go to the Citizens' Assembly, to make laws or to change rules. They could not send their sons to state schools, and never became rich or powerful.

Hoplites in battle

The **Helots** were slaves, who worked in the fields to produce food for the city. They had no rights at all, and were forced to work hard for no pay. They were owned by the state, and could not run away or change jobs. They could be forced into the army or the navy if there was a war. They could not own land, sell goods or argue with their masters. They had to do hard, back-breaking work, and could be beaten or even killed by the Spartiates.

In 464 BC the Helots tried to break free in a revolt, but this was crushed by the Spartan Army.

The Hoplites fighting the Helots

Government

Sparta was ruled by 2 Kings, a Council of 28 elders, 5 elected officials (**Ephors**), and the Citizens' Assembly.

The 2 Kings claimed to be related to Hercules, the great hero. Each King was allowed to lead the army, but he could not declare war or alter the size of the army. The Kings were considered to be the religious leaders of Sparta. But they could not make laws alone, or appoint their friends as members of the Council.

The Council advised the Kings or the Assembly, and said what it thought about laws and rules. The elders were chosen by the citizens. They had to be over 60 years old.

If a councillor had to be replaced, an election was held. Two senior councillors were shut in a room, and the candidates went out to the courtyard to present themselves to the citizens. The candidate who got the loudest cheer from the crowd (in the opinion of the 2 councillors) was elected.

The Ephors were the chief judges in Sparta. They discussed laws before they were presented to the Assembly. There were 5 Ephors; they were chosen each year by the Assembly.

The Assembly was open to every citizen over the age of 30. They met to talk about important matters, such as rules about citizenship or war, and to appoint generals.

Children

The Spartiates had very strict rules for the education of children, especially boys. All new-born babies were inspected by councillors, and if they were weak or sick, they were left on a hill to die. Boys stayed at home until they were 7 years old. Then they had to go to special schools, called **Agoge**.

Life at these schools was very tough indeed. Boys could not go home, and they had to do as they were told. At first, they were taught to read and write, but most of their time was spent in fitness or battle training. They could be beaten with a whip if they misbehaved.

When they reached the age of 12, training became really serious. Boys were not allowed to wear tunics, but had one cloak to wear all year round. They slept on the floor in large barrack rooms, and often had to get up early to go on a run or a march. Much of their time was spent on sport—not games like football or rugby, but wrestling, boxing and running. They also learnt how to use swords and other weapons.

They did not have much to eat. Sometimes they were told they could have no food at all, unless they stole some. Trained guards were put in charge of the food stores, and if any boys were caught stealing they were beaten. After about 10 years in a school like this, young men went straight into the Spartan Army.

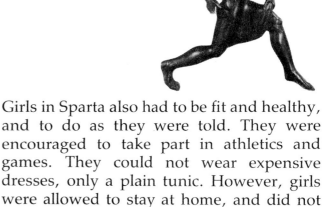

A bronze statue of a girl running, from Sparta

Girls in Sparta also had to be fit and healthy, and to do as they were told. They were encouraged to take part in athletics and games. They could not wear expensive dresses, only a plain tunic. However, girls were allowed to stay at home, and did not have to go to special schools. They could also walk freely around the streets, and had more rights than girls in other city-states.

---

1 Design a brochure to encourage people to come to Sparta. Only include the good things. Here are some ideas:
Slaves to do the work; very fair government (powerful and efficient yet wise and just); physical fitness; greater equality for girls than in other city-states; good education; beautiful scenery; efficient police; safety.

2 Write a letter from someone who has gone to Sparta and hates it. Only include the bad things.

3 What do you think about schools in Sparta?

4 What do you think the Spartans thought of the rich traders of Athens? Why were Athens and Sparta not likely to be very friendly?

Athens and Democracy

See Teachers' Notes page 6

The system of government and lawmaking in Athens was known as *democracy*. This meant that all the male citizens shared in choosing their leaders, and played some part in making laws and taking decisions. There was no King or Queen in Athens, but there was a Council of 500 men, and a large Assembly. This was a meeting open to free male citizens.

Other Greek city-states had different systems of government (see the table below). The diagrams opposite show how 2 of the systems worked.

Systems of government

SYSTEM	DESCRIPTION
Democracy	All male citizens share in making laws, by voting.
Monarchy	A king rules. He is the chief general, judge and priest. He inherits his power.
Oligarchy	A few rich people seize power, making rules that everybody else has to obey.
Tyranny	One man takes over by force, getting rid of the king. He makes all the laws.

- Copy the 2 diagrams into your book. Then, using the same symbols, draw your own diagrams to show the other 2 systems of government in the table. Colour the rulers red if they have come to power by force, or green if they inherited their position.

Key

In the diagrams below, this symbol stands for the **ruler**.

This symbol stands for the **people**.

TYRANNY

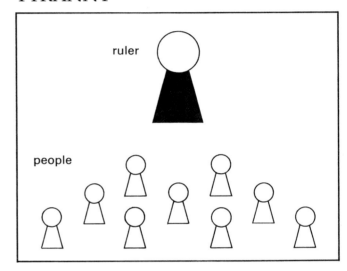

DEMOCRACY

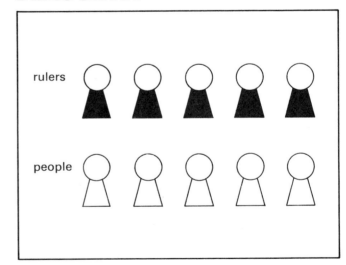

---

1 Which system of government do you think is fairest? Why?

2 Which system would work well during a war? Why?

The following exercise shows how democracy works. Your class has to produce a large poster to display. The whole class should follow the steps outlined below, using the methods of Athenian democracy to decide what the poster will look like. When you have finished, answer question 3.

3 What do you think were the main advantages and disadvantages of Athenian democracy?

ATHENS	YOUR CLASS
The **leaders** were elected as a group for one year. The Assembly chose men with experience and skill.	You elect one **judge** to sort out any arguments and make sure that the poster is finished. There will be 2 candidates—your teacher and the first volunteer. Each makes a short speech, then the class votes. The elected judge must carry out the decisions of the class.
Other **officials** (tax collectors, police chiefs etc.) were chosen by lot. Wooden counters with names on them were placed in a container, and one was picked out. No one could hold the same office twice. Juries for important trials were also chosen by lot.	You choose 3 **painters** by lot. The class write their names on pieces of paper. The judge draws out 3 of them.

All important decisions were taken by an **Assembly** of up to 6,000 men. Anyone could make a speech. Some speakers became famous. Once a year, any citizen who was unpopular could be 'ostracised'—made to leave the city for 10 years—if enough people voted against him.

You discuss these points:

1 What size will the poster be?
2 What should it show?
3 Which materials should be used?
4 Where should it be displayed?

A **president** must be chosen, by lot, for each discussion. Anyone can give his or her point of view, but can only speak for 3 minutes. The painters then finish the poster, while the class answers question 3, above.

An ostrakon—the small piece of broken pot on which a citizen wrote the name of the man he wanted to ostracise. This one reads 'Pericles son of Xanthippos'.

Athens

The Acropolis. 'Acropolis' means the highest place in the city. In earlier times, the Acropolis was used to defend Athens. The large building on the top is the Parthenon, the temple to Athena, the goddess of Athens

The city

The city of Athens was very different from Sparta. In Athens, trade and ships were very important, and there were many workshops and markets. Great temples and large public buildings were built to show the wealth of the city. Poets, teachers and writers were all highly respected in Athens.

Athens was the largest city in the state of Attica. The farming land around it was not very rich, although it did produce some wheat, and a lot of olives and wine. But there were marble quarries, and lead and silver mines. There was good red clay for pottery, and there were fine harbours. Athenian trading ships sailed all over the Mediterranean.

The League of Delos

Athens became powerful after the war against the Persians. The Athenian Navy managed to defeat the Persians at the Battle of Salamis in 480 BC. The Persians were then driven out of Greece. Other city-states and islands had joined Athens in an alliance against the Persians, known as the League of Delos. Athens began to ask for money from her friends and allies who wished to remain in the League and to be protected by the Athenian Navy. The less powerful among them had no choice, and paid. By 450 BC the League of Delos had become an Empire ruled by Athens.

Wealth

Athens was a very rich city. Many of its citizens were shopkeepers or traders, but only about 1% (2,000 people) were very rich. These men had made a lot of money from selling or making goods like wine, pottery and jewellery. They now owned great estates. When the city of Athens needed money for war, the rich citizens had to pay special taxes. Normally, the citizens paid no taxes at all.

The city's money came from 3 main sources:

A Ships that visited the port of Piraeus and unloaded cargoes had to pay a tax to the city.

B All non-citizens who lived in Athens had to pay taxes.

C The owners of silver mines and other industries had to pay rent to the city.

An Athenian coin. The owl was the symbol of Athena

Women

Women could not become rich or powerful in Athens. A woman could not go to the Assembly, serve in the law courts, or take part in business. Women were given away in marriage by their fathers, and their husbands gained a large amount of money (a dowry) on marrying. This money had to be returned to the bride's family if the marriage broke up, so most husbands looked after their wives. Women could not go out on their own. They had to stay at home and see to the household and the slaves. Nearly all wives baked bread, spun cloth and made clothes at home, with the help of slaves. An Athenian citizen, Apollodorus, declared, 'We have wives to give us children and look after our houses.'

Inside the Temple of Hephaistos, god of fire and metal-working

---

1 Rich citizens were expected to provide something of value for the city of Athens.
Select 2 things from the following list and explain why they would be valuable for the city.

- (a) A fully-manned trireme for a year
- (b) A new statue of a rich citizen to be placed in the market place
- (c) A public performance of a new play
- (d) Equipment and training for the city's athletes
- (e) A dozen female slaves

2 Write a short speech about life in Athens as if you were *one* of the following:
- (a) An Athenian woman
- (b) A Spartan soldier
- (c) An Athenian nobleman
- (d) An Athenian slave

Remember to include all the good and bad points about the city, and what you feel about the citizens.

3 Do you think that women were treated fairly in Athens and Sparta?

The Agora

The Agora was the heart of Athens. It was a large open space in the middle of the city. There were trees to give shade. Every day a market was held. Customers could buy many different sorts of vegetables, meat, fruit and other sorts of food. Many types of manufactured goods were on sale, particularly pottery, for which Greece was famous. Stalls which sold the same things were grouped together in one place. All around were workshops where customers could wander. Other traders sold from tables or trays which they carried around.

The Agora was a bustling, noisy and exciting place.

People flocked in from the surrounding countryside to bring their goods to market. The traders in the town brought their products to sell to the great crowds. Officials walked round the market to check that the prices were correct. Other officers made sure that the weights and measures being used were fair. There were officials to check that rubbish was not being left lying around, that the streets were not blocked and that people were not inconvenienced.

In the afternoons when the market was over, people would wander about talking and discussing politics. Sometimes there were official gatherings on a hill nearby. Crowds would gather to ostracise someone. They gave their pieces of broken pot to an official, and then stood with other members of their tribe to be counted. Sometimes, during festivals, processions, races and games were held there.

There were many impressive buildings around the edge of the Agora. These included law courts, temples, the army headquarters and the mint. Many of the important people of Athens could be seen going to and from their work.

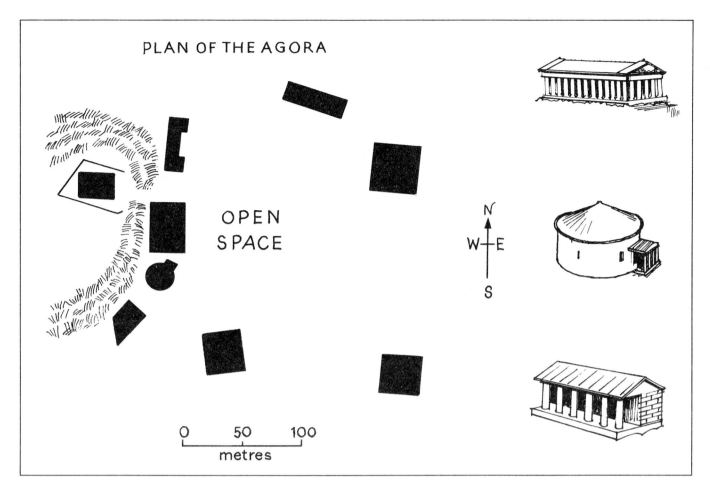

PLAN OF THE AGORA

OPEN
SPACE

N
W+E
S

0 50 100
metres

- Draw the plan of the Agora above, but much bigger. Label each building, using the table below to help you. Then put the symbols at the side of the plan in their right places. You could add some more symbols using your own ideas.

- You are a visitor to Athens. Write a description of a morning you spend in the Agora.

BUILDING	DESCRIPTION	POSITION
Stoa Poikile	Picture gallery and law court with room for juries of 501 people (a *stoa* was a long row of stalls, with open columns at the front)	North side
Tholos	Round building where the weights and measures officials met	West side
Strategeion	Army headquarters	West side – south of Tholos
Council house	Where the council of 500 met	West side – north of Tholos
Peristyle	Square building with roof held up by pillars to give a cool, shady area	N.E. corner
Temple of Hephaistos	God of fire and metal-working	On hill, west side
Stoa of Zeus	Office of Chief Archon in charge of festivals and other religious matters	N.W. corner
Mint	Where money was made	S.E. corner
Law courts	Main court with room for juries of 1001	South side – S.W. corner

Slavery in Athens

The total population of free people living in Athens in 450 BC was roughly 100,000. It is estimated that there were also about 100,000 slaves. Slaves were usually foreigners who had been kidnapped or captured in wars.

Some slaves were the property of the state. They could be road-menders, road-sweepers, public officials or clerks. Some worked in terrible conditions in the Athenian silver mines. Here they were whipped by overseers, and had to do back-breaking work until they died in utter misery.

Most slaves were the property of private citizens. Some worked in houses as cooks and servants, some were tanners, potters or metalworkers. Others were teachers or entertainers — acrobats and jugglers, for instance.

This painting, part of a pottery vase, shows slaves and their owners

A slave's life

Conditions for slaves varied according to their owners. Some were treated harshly, but others were like a member of the family they served. It made sense to treat them well because they were valuable property.

Owners might punish their slaves by beating them. Slaves might try to escape, but as they were often foreigners they would find it difficult to get very far. If they were caught, slaves could be branded.

Slaves could not become citizens, and neither could their children. They could not vote. They could earn their freedom if they worked well. But they would never be citizens.

Some slaves were given very responsible jobs managing workshops. Sometimes their owners paid them for working. Some slaves became bankers and a few became quite rich.

Some Greek writers show slaves as lazy and cheeky. Some authors gave advice on how to pick good slaves. Xenophon wrote, 'Pick the woman who seems least inclined to gluttony [greed], drink, sleep and running after men.'

This vase painting shows a slave being punished by his master

This is what a visitor to Athens said about slaves:

'There is a complete lack of discipline among slaves in Athens. You can't get away with hitting them there and don't expect them to give way for you in the Agora; they won't. I will tell you why this is. If the citizens were allowed to hit slaves it would cause chaos, since people would be forever hitting fellow citizens by mistake, thinking they were slaves. And that's because the people of Athens are no better dressed than the slaves, nor do they look any better off.'

Table 1

NATIONALITY	VALUE
Thracian female	165 drachma
Thracian female	135 dr.
Thracian male	170 dr.
Syrian male	240 dr.
Carian male	105 dr.
Illyrian male	161 dr.
Thracian female	220 dr.
Thracian male	115 dr.
Scythian male	144 dr.
Illyrian male	144 dr.
Colchian male	153 dr.
Carian male (young)	174 dr.
Carian infant	72 dr.
Syrian male	301 dr.
Maltese male	106 dr.
Lydian female	170 dr.

The slaves in Table 1 were sold by public auction in Athens in 414 BC. They had belonged to a nobleman.

These slaves were sold for a lot of money. It is very difficult to say what the sums are worth in today's money. In Ancient Greece you could buy a loaf of bread for 1 obol, and there were 6 obols in a drachma.

1 How many slaves did this nobleman own?

2 Which slave was the most valuable?

3 What could you say generally about the value of male, female and child slaves?

4 Look at Table 2. Why did Plato and Nikias keep slaves?

Table 2

OWNER	SLAVES
Nikias	1000 (miners)
Timarchos	10 (one weaver and the rest shoemakers)
Plato	5 (personal attendants)

■■■

Part of a tombstone showing a slave attending her mistress

Female slaves did the housework in large Athenian homes. The Greek poet Homer wrote this description of a woman telling the slaves what to do:

'Get to work now, girls! Some of you start sweeping and sprinkling the floors, and put purple rugs on all the chairs. . . . Others can sponge the tables down, and clean the mixing-bowls and all the inlaid silverware. The rest of you, go to the well and fetch water. Be as quick as you can; today is a holiday, and our noble guests will be here soon!'

1 Why were slaves who worked in the silver mines so important for Athens?

2 Compare the jobs done by female and male slaves. Were slaves in Athens better off than the Helots in Sparta?

3 Imagine you live in Athens in about 400 BC. You have 2 slaves and you have decided to free one of them. Read the descriptions of the slaves below and write a few sentences explaining which one you have decided to free and why.

Slave A — an old man. He has served you faithfully all your life. He runs your very profitable pottery workshop. He will be hard to replace.

Slave B — a man of middle age. An excellent craftsman. One of the best pottery painters in Athens. He is strong and very aggressive. He has caused some trouble recently.

4 It was possible to free slaves but still make them work for you and pay you money. Does this make any difference to the decision you have just made (question 3)?

5 Write 3 sentences describing the jobs being done by the slaves in the pictures on these pages.

43

Athens and Sparta at War

See Teachers' Notes page 6

In 431 BC Athens was the strongest of the city-states, with an Empire of islands and cities in the Aegean Sea. The Empire paid tribute to Athens, usually in money and ships. The Athenian Navy controlled the Empire.

Other city-states became jealous and frightened of the growing power of Athens. Two states in particular, Corinth and Sparta, wanted to put an end to it. Sparta had a very strong army and had organised some of the city-states into an alliance.

In the spring of 431 BC, 300 Hoplites (foot-soldiers) from Thebes, one of Sparta's allies, attacked Plataea. Plataea was an ally of Athens. The war had begun. It lasted until 404 BC.

- This game shows the progress of the war between Athens and Sparta. Players take the part of the Athenians. Your teacher will tell you how to play. Players try to build up enough strength to defeat Sparta. When you have finished the game, answer the questions on page 45.

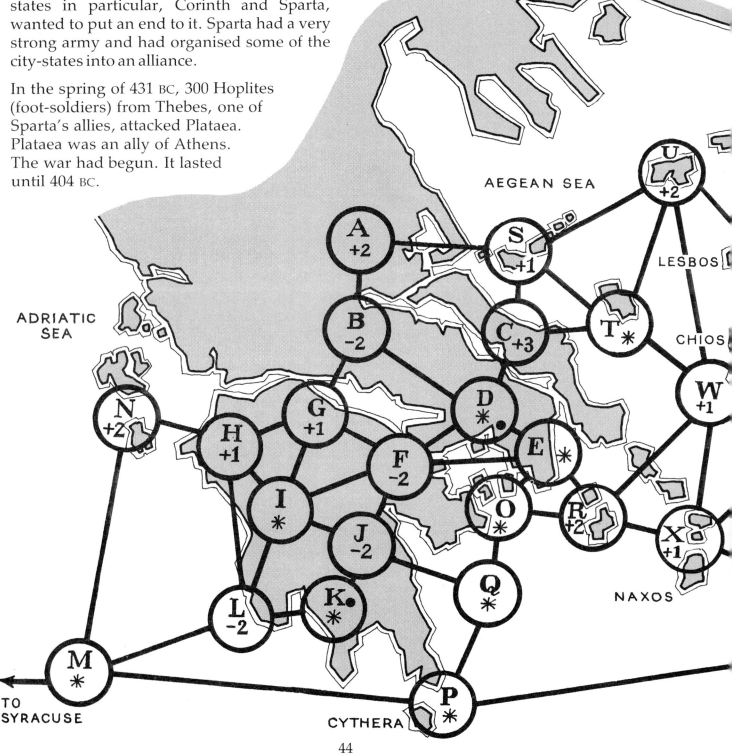

AEGEAN SEA

ADRIATIC SEA

LESBOS

CHIOS

NAXOS

TO SYRACUSE

CYTHERA

Information to help you play

Sparta (K)

Sparta will fight the war mostly on land. Spartan armies will attack the allies of Athens. They will march to Athens to try to capture the city. They will take many slaves and destroy fields and crops. This will weaken Athens and make Sparta stronger.

Sparta starts the game with a strength of 2. This strength increases by 1 point for each round that you play which does not capture Sparta. You keep a running total of Sparta's strength on the score-card which your teacher will give you.

Athens (D)

Pericles, your leader, has decided that the best way to fight the war is to keep everyone inside the city. The Spartans are not good at besieging cities. Athens can be supplied by sea, so everyone will be safe. The Spartans may give up and go home.

In the meantime, the Athenian Navy will visit different parts of the Empire and gather as much tribute [money] and support as possible. Raids will be made on Spartan land. It would be good to start a new Empire in the Adriatic Sea to the west. The young Athenians do not like the plan much. They prefer more action with glorious battles.

Athens begins the game with a strength of 4. Your strength increases as tribute is collected but decreases as battles are fought.

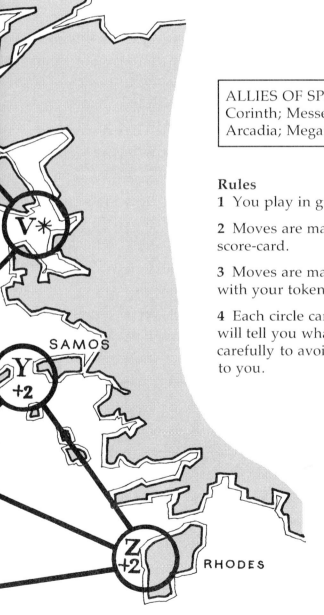

ALLIES OF SPARTA	ALLIES OF ATHENS
Corinth; Messenia; Elis; Arcadia; Megara; Boetia	Delos; Chios; Lesbos; Samos; Naxos; many smaller islands; colonies in Asia Minor

Rules

1 You play in groups of 2 or 3, using 1 board and 1 token per group.

2 Moves are made 1 at a time. Each move must be recorded on the score-card.

3 Moves are made from circle to circle along the lines shown. You start with your token on **D**. You can visit circles in any order.

4 Each circle can be visited only once, except Athens (**D**). Your teacher will tell you what happens when you visit Athens. Work out your route carefully to avoid being trapped. The number of circles you visit is up to you.

1 Who were the main allies of Athens?

2 Why were the Athenians less successful on land?

3 What was one bad result of Pericles' plan of keeping the citizens in Athens?

4 What effect did the attack on Syracuse have on Athens?

5 Why did Sparta become stronger as the war went on?

6 Why was Sparta so hard to defeat?

7 Use your moves in the game to explain the progress of Athens during the war.

The Roman Empire

See Teachers' Notes page 8

Rome grew from a small village into a large city which controlled the whole of Italy. At the height of its power, Rome ruled an Empire of several million square miles — the whole of the area shown on the map. The Roman Army, divided into *Legions*, controlled all this land, while governors, lawyers and civil servants all made sure that everything ran smoothly. One poet said that Rome had 'made one City, where once was a World'.

- You can find out how the Romans built up their Empire by playing this game, which your teacher will explain. After the game, draw the map. Then write a short account of the growth of your Empire.

Rules

1 You begin in Rome with 2 legions.

2 Each time you conquer a province you gain 2 extra legions. You gain no extra legions in Egypt, or if you go to the same place twice.

3 The number of legions needed to conquer a province is shown by the numbers in the circles.

4 You cannot conquer a province unless you have enough legions.

5 You can only enter a new province from an area you have already conquered, e.g. you cannot enter Asia Minor until you have conquered Italy and Macedonia.

6 Provinces are divided from each other by dotted lines or by natural barriers like mountains and rivers (see key).

7 Keep a careful note of the stages by which you build up your Empire and the growing size of the Roman Army. Each move you make equals roughly 50 years of real time.

KEY

～ RIVER

MOUNTAINS

--- BORDERS BETWEEN PROVINCES

④ NUMBER OF LEGIONS NEEDED TO CONQUER

ASIA MINOR

SYRIA

JUDAEA

EGYPT

What is known about the provinces

Asia Minor, Syria, Judaea	Difficult countries to fight in. Hot and mountainous. A long way from Rome.
Britain (Britannia)	Very little known. Rumours of savage tribes fighting one another. Has valuable metals like tin and gold.
Carthage	Rich and powerful city with a large navy. Wants to take over the Mediterranean. Rome not safe until Carthage beaten.
Dacia	Mountains and forests make it hard to attack. Fierce tribes which keep raiding Macedonia. Great wealth.
Egypt	Once a great power but now fairly weak. Very rich with many luxury goods.
Gaul (Gallia)	Contains savage fighters and hunters who like to raid Italy. No king or organised government. Tribes often fight each other. A rich area.
Germany (Germania)	Mountains and forests make it hard to attack. Hordes of savage warriors who can join together constantly attack northern Gaul.
Macedonia (part of Greece)	Once a great power but now quite weak. Many trading connections.
Italy (Italia), South Gaul	A mixture of small tribes who do not like Rome's growing power. Etruscans, Latins and Greeks. Few in number and poorly organised. They have many skills, like pottery-making, building etc.
Spain (Hispania)	Disorganised, primitive tribes. Used as a base by Carthage. Barbarian lands. Trackless wastes containing untold numbers of ferocious warriors.

The Roman Emperor

See Teachers' Notes page 8

After 27 BC Rome was ruled by an Emperor — one man who held great power. Some Emperors, like Augustus and Theodosius, ruled for over 40 years. But usually an Emperor's reign was much shorter, as there were many problems to be faced, and many rivals all hoping to take the Emperor's place. In the year AD 69 there were 4 Emperors— Galba, Otho, Vitellius and Vespasian. This set of exercises looks at some of the problems faced by one Emperor—*Claudius*, who ruled from AD 41 to 54.

The Emperor Claudius

Background and personality

The Emperor Caligula was murdered by his own bodyguards in AD 41. The new Emperor was his uncle, Claudius. Many Romans were very surprised by this, because they felt that Claudius was inexperienced, and he was often ill.

DECISION 1

You have just taken over as Emperor. You are told that the Senators [politicians] don't like you and want to get rid of you by helping rebels in other parts of the Empire.

What should you do?
1 Make a speech in the Senate asking for help.
2 Send in the army to arrest the Senators.
3 Leave Rome and give up being Emperor.
4 Do nothing.

This would help ☐

DECISION 2

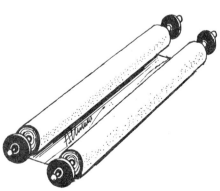

Two British chiefs have written to you asking for help against Caratacus and Tugodumnus, 2 British leaders who have refused to be friends with Rome. The Romans attacked Britain many years ago, but left soon after.

What should you do?
1 Write a letter to Caratacus.
2 Send the army to Syria.
3 Ignore the letter and leave Britain alone.
4 Send an army to invade Britain.

This would help ☐

48

There were, however, 2 very good reasons why Claudius became Emperor:

A His family. He was related to Augustus, the first Emperor.

B His friends. He was helped by the men of the Praetorian Guard, the most powerful soldiers in the Roman Army. They were the Emperor's bodyguards. Perhaps they felt it would be easy to control Claudius.

Suetonius, a Roman writer, said this about Claudius:

'Nearly the whole of his childhood and youth was so troubled by various diseases that he grew dull-witted and had little physical strength; and on reaching the age at which he should have won a magistracy or chosen a private career, he was considered by his family unable to do either.
Claudius had a certain majesty and dignity of presence. . . though tall, well built, with a handsome face, a fine head of white hair and a firm neck, he stumbled as he walked owing to the weakness of his knees, and he had several disagreeable traits. These included an uncontrolled laugh, and a horrible habit, under the stress of anger, of slobbering at the mouth and running at the nose, a stammer, and a persistent nervous tic of the head. . . .'

The Emperor was very powerful, but was always in danger of being overthrown or assassinated. He had to try to please the most important people in the Empire—the Senators [politicians], who met in the Senate, the army, and the people of Rome.

- The table below shows 4 important decisions Claudius had to take as Emperor.
  Copy each problem into your book, and underline the decision that you would take as Emperor. Then, in a box like the ones in the table, write **army**, **people** or **Senators** to show which group of people would have gained most from your decision. Your teacher will tell you about the decisions Claudius actually took. You should then be able to answer the questions below.

1 Why did Claudius become Emperor?

2 Describe 2 problems faced by Claudius.

3 Write a letter to an enemy of Claudius pointing out his faults.

4 Was Claudius a good Emperor?

5 Find out about any other Roman Emperors and their successes.

DECISION 3

The people of Rome are very angry because bread prices have gone up. Many people cannot afford a loaf of bread. (Note: Bread is the main meal for poor people.)

What should you do?
1 Give the army's supplies of bread to Rome.
2 Build a new port to take more grain ships.
3 Tell all bakers to work for no money.

This would help

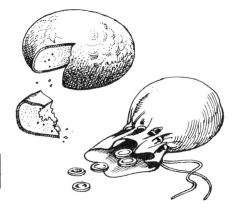

DECISION 4

Several friends have told you that your wife, Messalina, has been plotting to kill you. They have also said that you cannot trust your advisers.

What should you do?
1 Arrest your wife and your advisers.
2 Arrest all your friends.
3 Go on holiday.
4 Ask the Senate for help and advice.

This would help

The Legions 1

The power of Rome was based on the Roman Army. The army was like a well-oiled machine. All soldiers had to supply their own weapons (javelins and swords) and armour. They had to be taught to fight together. They spent hours every week learning how to use their weapons, and practising marching, drill, parades and other exercises. This was to make sure that each soldier knew his own place in the legion, the basic unit of the Roman Army. In 200 BC there were 4 legions in the Roman Army. By AD 50 there were 28. Each legion had its own commander (known as a *legate*) and its own base somewhere in the Empire.

A legion contained about 5,500 legionaries divided into 10 cohorts.

The Roman Army defeated the armies of many other nations. The tribes of western Europe, known as the Barbarians, were among their fiercest opponents.

The passage below is based on a description of the Barbarians by Tacitus, a Roman historian.

Each cohort had its own standard-bearer

'Most carry spears with short and narrow blades which can be used either at close quarters or in long-range fighting. Their horsemen are content with a shield and one spear, but the foot-soldiers also use javelins. Each carries several, and they throw them to great distances, being naked or lightly dressed in short cloaks. The commanders rely on the admiration they win by pushing forward in front of their troops. The squadrons and divisions are each composed of one family or clan. Close by them too are their nearest and dearest, so that they can hear the shrieks of their women-folk and the wailing of their children.'

Right. This is part of the decoration on Trajan's Column in Rome. The Emperor Trajan added many provinces to the Roman Empire. His soldiers put up many bridges and buildings. In the lower part of the picture you can see soldiers marching over a bridge of boats

1 Copy these sentences into your book. After each sentence write 'B' if you think it applies only to a Barbarian soldier, or 'R' if you think it applies only to a Roman soldier. Write 'Both' if you think it applies to both Romans and Barbarians.

  (a) He has very good armour.
  (b) He has only one type of weapon.
  (c) He fights on foot.
  (d) He listens very carefully to commands.
  (e) He will fight to the death.
  (f) He is very well trained.
  (g) He throws a javelin.
  (h) He marches in close formations.
  (i) He takes his family into battle.
  (j) He may become a centurion.

Write a paragraph comparing a Roman soldier with a Barbarian soldier. You can add drawings.

2 The division of a legion into cohorts meant that the soldiers could move into different formations very easily. For instance, when attacking a square of foot-soldiers, the legion might form into an arrowhead shape.

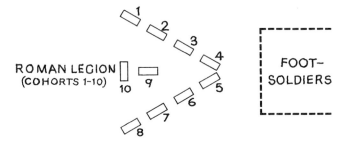

(a) Draw a diagram to show a legion in the following formations:
  (i) A square, with cohorts 1–8 forming the sides, and cohorts 9 and 10 in reserve.
  (ii) Cohorts 1–8 forming a crescent in front of cohorts 9 and 10.

(b) Explain which of these formations you would use against:
- (i) lines of charging elephants,
- (ii) a fort or town,
- (iii) horsemen.

(c) Why was drill so important in the Roman Army?

(d) Why do you think the Roman Army was so successful?
(Try to give 3 or 4 possible reasons)

3 You are a Barbarian sent to spy on the Roman Army. Use the information on this page and the scenes from the picture to write a report on its organisation, and the soldiers you have seen.

The Legions 2

See Teachers' Notes page 8

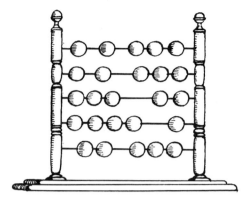

Claudius has decided to invade Britain. He has built many ships and he wants to take the strongest army possible. Unfortunately, he is rather short of money, because he has to pay all the other soldiers who are guarding the borders of the Empire.

- You have been given the job of working out the best army for Claudius to take. Follow the 6 steps to see how you do it.

1 Copy the abacus graph above. It shows all the money Claudius has to spend. (This is represented by the 25 beads. They are all of equal value, although on a real abacus they would not be.)

THE BRITONS

Foot-soldiers: Fight mainly with swords and small shields. They are very fierce. They fight better in single combat. They cannot swing their swords properly in the thick of battle and they wear no armour. They are not well disciplined and may run away if things go badly.

War chariots: Carry 2 or 3 warriors, who throw spears from the moving chariot. Warriors can also dismount and fight with swords. A line of chariots can break up a line of advancing soldiers

THE ROMANS

Legions: Legionaries join the army for 25 years. They train every day. They are well disciplined and reliable. They wear body armour and carry large shields. They each have 2 javelins which they can throw accurately up to 30 metres. They use a short stabbing sword (*gladius*). They can use many different formations in battle.

> **1 legion (5,500 men) costs:** —Ⓛ—Ⓛ—

Cavalry: Useful for chasing enemies who are running away, carrying messages, and searching for food. Without stirrups, they are unsteady in the saddle when attacking determined foot-soldiers or chariots. There are usually 40 legionaries to one horseman.

> **500 men and horses cost:** —Ⓗ—

2 Check what the Romans know about the Britons and how they fight (see also page 47).

3 Read about how the Romans fight.

4 The cost of each part of the Roman Army is shown in beads. (In this case each bead is worth several thousand silver coins.)

5 To hire any part of the Roman Army, you will write its letter into the correct number of blank beads on your abacus graph.

e.g. 1 legion = —(L)-(L)—
   2 legions = —(L)-(L)-(L)-(L)—
   3 weeks' food = —(F)-(F)-(F)—

6 You should use all the beads on the abacus but it is up to you to decide *how* to use them.

When you have followed these steps, you can answer the questions:

1 Write down exactly how many legions, auxiliary legions, cavalry, elephants and catapults, and how much food Claudius should take.

2 Write a letter to Claudius explaining why you have chosen this army and its equipment. Explain how the Britons fight and how the Romans fight. Explain why the Romans will win. You can illustrate your letter.

3 Ask your teacher to show you how a real abacus works.

- - -

(on foot or on horseback), and can move warriors around the battlefield. Only a few British chieftains and warriors have war chariots.

Hill forts: Strong earthworks that can hold thousands of Britons. The gateways can be blocked and the high walls make the hill forts hard to capture.

Maiden Castle, a hill fort in Dorset, seen from the air. You can still visit Maiden Castle today

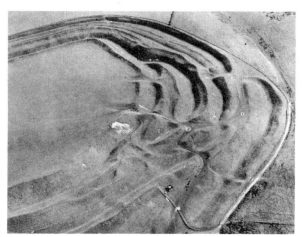

- - -

Auxiliaries: Come from all over the Empire. They have special skills—there are archers, slingers, spearmen and so on. They support the legions and do all the jobs the legions cannot. There are usually the same number of auxiliaries in an army as there are legionaries.

> **1 legion of auxiliaries (5,500 men) costs:** —(A)-(A)—

Elephants: Claudius has a special ship which carries 40 elephants. They are hard to kill, fierce in battle but difficult to control. They may frighten the Britons who have never seen elephants before.

> **40 elephants cost:** —(E)—

Catapults: These giant catapults shoot rocks or huge spears. They are made of wood and powered by twisted ropes. They can smash down walls and gates.

> **200 catapults cost:** —(C)—

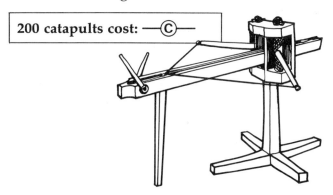

Food: May be hard to find if the Britons keep attacking.

> **1 week's food for the whole army costs:** —(F)—

A Soldier's Day

Roman legions were sent to all parts of the Empire to protect the borders and control the provinces. In AD 68 there were 3 legions stationed in Britain. There was Legion II at Gloucester, Legion IX at Lincoln and Legion XX near Shrewsbury. Altogether there were about 15,000 Roman soldiers in Britain.

These soldiers spent their time in a base camp like the one shown opposite. Detachments were sent to do a tour of duty on Hadrian's Wall or at the other trouble spots. But many soldiers did not see any action while on duty. This game will show you what an ordinary day may have been like.

Drill and discipline were very important for the Roman soldiers in Britain. They had to be ready and trained to fight at a moment's notice. Play the game, then answer the questions on page 55.

Rules
Make a suitable token to move round the board. Toss a coin to move. Heads: move to the next black semi-circle. Tails: move to the next white semi-circle. Record only the things that happen to you.

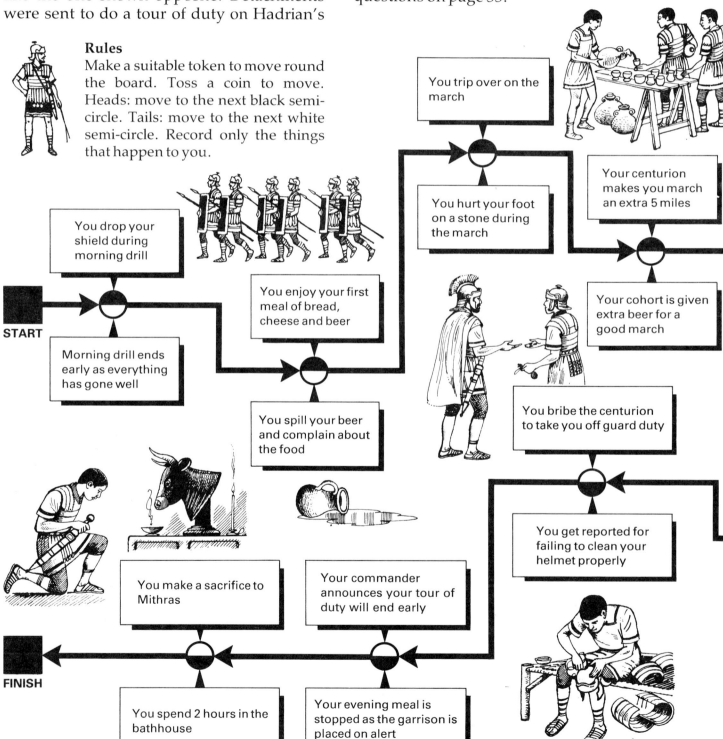

You trip over on the march

Your centurion makes you march an extra 5 miles

You hurt your foot on a stone during the march

You drop your shield during morning drill

You enjoy your first meal of bread, cheese and beer

Your cohort is given extra beer for a good march

START

Morning drill ends early as everything has gone well

You spill your beer and complain about the food

You bribe the centurion to take you off guard duty

You get reported for failing to clean your helmet properly

You make a sacrifice to Mithras

Your commander announces your tour of duty will end early

FINISH

You spend 2 hours in the bathhouse

Your evening meal is stopped as the garrison is placed on alert

54

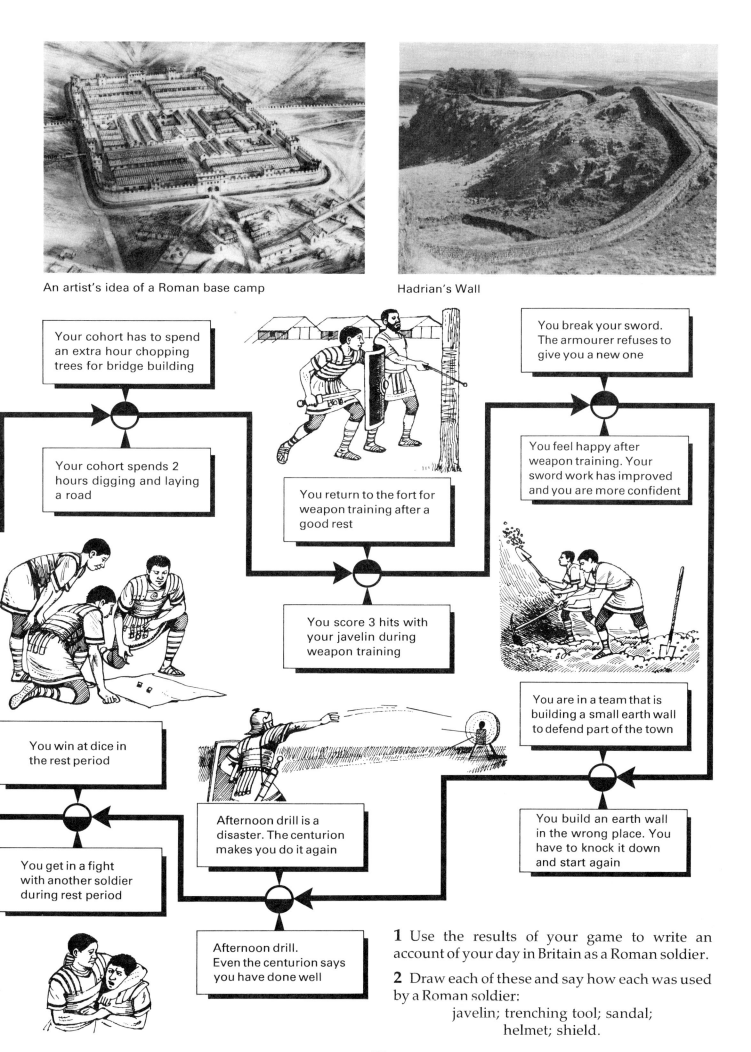

An artist's idea of a Roman base camp

Hadrian's Wall

Your cohort has to spend an extra hour chopping trees for bridge building

Your cohort spends 2 hours digging and laying a road

You break your sword. The armourer refuses to give you a new one

You feel happy after weapon training. Your sword work has improved and you are more confident

You return to the fort for weapon training after a good rest

You score 3 hits with your javelin during weapon training

You win at dice in the rest period

You get in a fight with another soldier during rest period

Afternoon drill is a disaster. The centurion makes you do it again

You are in a team that is building a small earth wall to defend part of the town

You build an earth wall in the wrong place. You have to knock it down and start again

Afternoon drill. Even the centurion says you have done well

1 Use the results of your game to write an account of your day in Britain as a Roman soldier.

2 Draw each of these and say how each was used by a Roman soldier:
javelin; trenching tool; sandal; helmet; shield.

55

The City of Rome

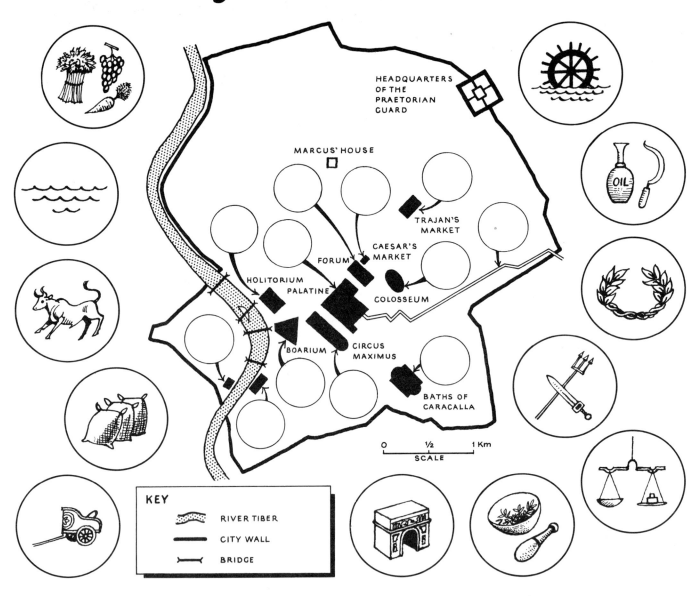

Marcus is a rich Roman citizen. He lives in Rome in the year AD 100. We can get to know Rome well if we follow him for one day.

Like most Romans Marcus gets up at dawn. After having some porridge and wine he leaves his villa to inspect his various businesses.

Four of his slaves carry him in his litter through the crowded streets. The litter is jostled by throngs of people. More than a million people live in Rome and all of them seem to be going to the same place as Marcus, the Forum. This is the centre of Rome. It is a splendid open space surrounded by temples, magnificent statues and triumphal arches. The Roman Senate meets here. Off to one side of the Forum is Caesar's Market, where all kinds of spices can be bought.

The litter pushes through the crowds and the slaves turn north-east to Trajan's market. Here there are lots of little shops. Marcus buys a brooch for his wife's birthday.

Marcus tells his slaves to head for the river. Soon they pass the great Colosseum where gladiators fight to entertain the crowds. The amphitheatre seats 50,000 people. When it is very hot a cloth roof is drawn over it. Up to his right Marcus can see the Palatine Hill. The palace of the Emperor is on the top.

The litter passes under the aqueduct built by the Emperor Claudius which brings fresh water to the people of Rome.

Before long they come to the Forum Baorium. There is a great noise and smell from all the cattle which have been driven into the city to be sold. Marcus orders his litter to stop in the Forum Holitorium. He speaks to an important slave who has brought 2 cartloads of vegetables from Marcus' market garden outside Rome. The slave says that business is good.

The next stop is Marcus' warehouse. This is near the river Tiber. Barges, pulled by slaves, come from the port of Ostia. Goods come to Rome from all over the Empire. Marcus inspects a cargo of corn which has just arrived from Egypt. Across the river he can see his flour mill. There are over 250 mills in Rome but only about 20 are powered by water like his.

By now Marcus is feeling tired so he is carried to the baths. He leaves his toga with an attendant and then swims and sweats in the hot room. A slave massages him with oil and scrapes the dirt off him with a scraper. When he is quite clean Marcus wanders about the other rooms in the baths. He buys some delicious pastries from a stall. When he decides to leave he is furious to find that his toga has been stolen, and he has to go home wearing the ragged one the thief has left behind.

On his way home Marcus passes the Circus Maximus. This is the chariot racing stadium. It holds over 250,000 people. Chariot racing is very exciting to watch. There are lots of

The Colosseum today

crashes. Marcus always bets heavily on his favourite team, the Greens.

Just past the Circus the slaves turn north towards Marcus' house. They pass Caesar's Market. Marcus is a bit late for dinner but everyone expects that in Rome, where there are no accurate clocks. Anyway, his wife is very pleased with her brooch.

1 Copy or trace the plan of Rome. Use the description of Marcus' journey to help you put the small drawings in their right circles.

2 Draw what you think Marcus' litter might have looked like.

3 Make a list of some of the good things and bad things about living in Rome at this time.

An artist's idea of the Roman forum as it looked in Marcus' time

Life at the Top

See Teachers' Notes page 8

Rich Roman citizens led an enjoyable life. They could make a great deal of money in a number of ways—selling slaves, or food to the army, or gold or silver from their mines. Many bought great estates in the country as well as town houses. Cicero paid 875,000 denarii for his town house. These large houses often had central heating and private baths. In the country, slaves worked in the fields as well as in the house.

A sculpture showing a Roman housewife shopping

A rich lady would have slave girls to dress her, comb her hair and wait on her. Rich families could afford many slaves and entertainments. One favourite entertainment was the dinner party. The guests were served with many kinds of meat, fish and fruit, and wine of the highest quality. They

A dinner party

spent hours eating and talking between courses. Many Roman citizens felt that after-dinner conversation was an art.

Several writers wrote books about how to impress other people by talking. But they warned their readers not to be rude about the Emperor in case it was reported.

There was a character in a book by the author Petronius called Trimalchio. He was a rich Roman, and his story was based on the careers of several real people.

Trimalchio came as a slave from Asia at the age of 14. He was sold to a Roman Senator and became a steward. When his master died, Trimalchio was given his freedom and half the estate. He was now very rich.

He bought 5 ships with cargoes of wine. The ships set out to take the wine to Rome, but all of them were wrecked in a storm. However, Trimalchio's wife, Fortunata, sold all her jewellery and clothes, and gave the money to Trimalchio. He used it to buy more ships and cargoes. This time the voyage was completed, and Trimalchio made a huge profit.

Trimalchio then bought and sold land, using his profits to buy slaves at the slave market. Soon he became a millionaire, and began to lend money to many Roman citizens. He then retired, built a large villa, and began to buy different estates. He boasted that he hoped to be able to travel from Sicily to Africa without leaving his own land.

- How would you spend money if you were a Roman businessman? You start with a capital of 5 units. Place a counter (e.g. a coin) on one of the starting squares below. You can move up the ladders one square at a time, adding or subtracting the number shown to see what happens to your money after each move. You can move across to another ladder by following one of the arrows. This counts as one move. You must stop after 10 moves. When you stop, you multiply the amount of money you now have by the number in the square you are in to calculate your final profit. The player with the biggest profit is the winner.

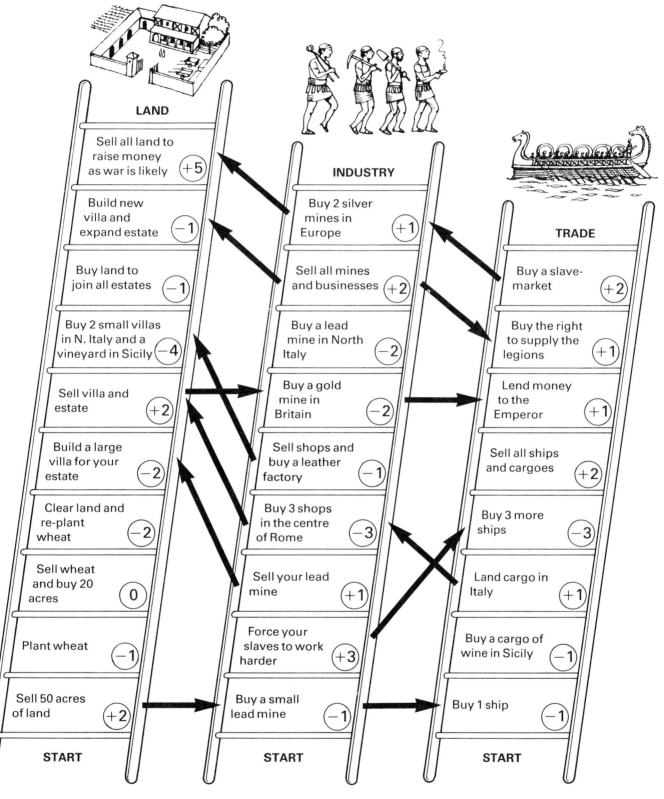

LAND

Square	Value
Sell all land to raise money as war is likely	+5
Build new villa and expand estate	−1
Buy land to join all estates	−1
Buy 2 small villas in N. Italy and a vineyard in Sicily	−4
Sell villa and estate	+2
Build a large villa for your estate	−2
Clear land and re-plant wheat	−2
Sell wheat and buy 20 acres	0
Plant wheat	−1
Sell 50 acres of land	+2

START

INDUSTRY

Square	Value
Buy 2 silver mines in Europe	+1
Sell all mines and businesses	+2
Buy a lead mine in North Italy	−2
Buy a gold mine in Britain	−2
Sell shops and buy a leather factory	−1
Buy 3 shops in the centre of Rome	−3
Sell your lead mine	+1
Force your slaves to work harder	+3
Buy a small lead mine	−1

START

TRADE

Square	Value
Buy a slave-market	+2
Buy the right to supply the legions	+1
Lend money to the Emperor	+1
Sell all ships and cargoes	+2
Buy 3 more ships	−3
Land cargo in Italy	+1
Buy a cargo of wine in Sicily	−1
Buy 1 ship	−1

START

Notes

1 You have 10 moves.

2 In round 10 multiply your capital by the number in the square where you finish.

3 Going along an arrow counts as one move.

4 You start with 5 units. Keep a running total as you go along.

59

Life at the Bottom: Slavery

See Teachers' Notes page 8

A slave had a hard life. Slaves were usually prisoners captured in war, but some were people who were kidnapped in Italy.

Slaves were sold at a slave-market. They were put on show, naked, with a notice around their necks. Anyone with money bought them. They usually cost between 500 and 1,500 denarii. They became the property of their new owner and had to work for no money.

They could be treated badly and beaten. Any slave who ran away could be put to death. If a slave killed the master, all the other slaves in the household, perhaps as many as 400 people, would be killed. Slaves could not argue with their masters, as they were just property, like a horse or a piece of furniture.

Both men and women were sold as slaves. Often the most expensive slaves were young boys. Slaves were sometimes well educated, especially those from Greece. These slaves were usually bought by rich people and worked as teachers, clerks or housekeepers.

Women slaves could be hairdressers, dressmakers, cooks and servants for rich women. Slaves also worked in small workshops, making leather goods, silver goods, pots, pans and weapons. The hardest work was usually in the mines where slaves had to dig deep underground. They used hand tools and worked in hot, cramped conditions. Little attention was paid to safety and there were many accidents. Slaves also did all the digging, ploughing and other farm work on large estates.

Slaves were used for building, road-making and other public works. Hundreds of public slaves were attached to the Consuls of Rome. They also acted as clerks and tax-collectors. One very important job done by public slaves was repairing the 8 aqueducts which supplied the city with fresh water.

A statue of a slave boy with a lamp. He is waiting until his owner is ready to go home

Often slaves tried to run away, but this was difficult because they had no one to help them, and many of them did not speak Latin very well. At one time, Spartacus, who had been a gladiator, formed a slave army. It defeated the Roman Army in a great battle. The promise of freedom was enough to make thousands of slaves join him, but the revolt was crushed and the survivors were crucified.

60

● Imagine you are looking for runaway slaves in Rome. Read this information and then answer the questions.

Tiberius

This man was found sleeping in a back alley in Rome. He has no shoes and is dressed in rags. His beard and hair have been cut recently. His hands are smooth with long fingernails. His leather bag contains a wax tablet and 2 pens.

He says that he has just returned to Rome after 10 years service with Legion XIX on the Rhine frontier. He cannot remember the names of his commander or centurion.

He says he is a fine craftsman able to make fine pottery and silverware, but he could not find a shop that needed his help. His parents settled in Greece many years ago but they are both dead now. He speaks with a Greek accent and does not know his way around the city very well.

Gracchus

He is a young man aged about 20. He started a fight in a baker's shop. He has very muscular arms and chest but he limps badly. He has many scars on his back and shoulders. One of his ears is missing.

He cannot read or write and seems to have great difficulty in understanding what is said to him. However, he is clearly not deaf or dumb. His hands are very worn and gnarled. He has no fingernails. There are specks of silver dust and mud on his clothes. He does not know anything about the laws of the city and says he did not recognise the official and soldiers who stopped him fighting.

1 For each man make a list of 5 points which you feel show he is an escaped slave.

2 Why might slaves want to run away?

3 What happened to runaway slaves?

4 What jobs did public slaves do?

5 Who was Spartacus? How successful was he?

6 Copy the table below (yours will be bigger). Choose words from the list of places to fill in the 'Where from?' column. Choose words from the list of slaves to fill in the 'Slaves involved' column. Your teacher may discuss other objects with you.

7 Were slaves an important part of Roman life? Give reasons for your answer.

How to get what you want in Rome

WHAT?	WHERE FROM?	SLAVES INVOLVED
A loaf of bread		
A glass of water		
A silver jug		

Places: aqueduct; silver mine; wheatfield; fountain; mill; shop; bakery.

Slaves: public slave; shop slave; household slave; mine slave; field slave.

The Games in Rome

A chariot race in the Circus Maximus

Ordinary Roman citizens lived in brick-built houses and flats in crowded streets. They hardly ever went away from Rome.

On festivals and public holidays Roman citizens went to the games. In the arena, prisoners of war and criminals were put to death. Some were made to fight each other, and some were thrown to wild animals. There were also highly trained professional gladiators who were taught at special gladiator schools.

The games were violent and spectacular. Paying for games to be held became a way of getting the support of the Roman people. Emperors held games that became bigger and bigger and more and more bloodthirsty. In AD 80, for instance, the Emperor Titus opened the Colosseum with a series of games that were supposed to last for 100 days. These games included fights between hundreds of men and thousands of wild animals, which had been captured on hunting expeditions to North Africa. There was even a naval battle when the whole arena was flooded.

Another very popular spectacle was the chariot races held in the Circus Maximus. There were usually 4 teams in a race. They were called the Reds, Greens, Whites and Blues. The chariots were very light and pulled by teams of 2 or 4 horses. They raced round the track 7 times.

The chariot drivers were usually trained slaves. They wrapped the reins around their bodies. Each driver carried a sharp knife to cut himself free if there was a crash. Racing often went on all day, with heats leading up to the finals in the evening. The winners received a purse of gold and were treated like heroes.

The citizens placed bets on their favourite teams. They waved coloured scarves to support the drivers.

Gladiator fights

Gladiators were slaves trained to fight to the death in the arena. They had different sorts of weapons and armour to make the fights more exciting. The best known gladiators were the swordsmen (*secutores*) and netmen (*retarii*). The swordsmen wore armour and carried large shields and short swords. The netmen were armed with a sharp, 3-pronged spear (trident) and a large net. The netman threw his net over his opponent, who became entangled in it. The netman then tried to stab his opponent with his spear.

Often 2 teams of gladiators started a contest, but at the end there would only be one man left standing. The crowd cheered and grew very excited during the contests. Wounded gladiators could appeal to the spectators for mercy, but often only death would satisfy them.

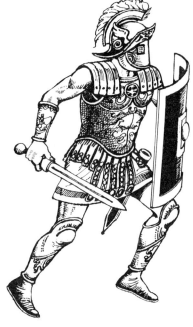

```
G  A  C  S  G  N  M  A  E
P  L  H  A  L  H  A  R  B
T  S  A  N  G  R  E  E  N
R  H  R  D  N  E  T  N  O
I  I  I  E  I  T  S  A  I
D  E  O  O  D  A  J  K  L
E  L  T  R  G  R  T  P  Y
N  D  Y  A  D  I  L  O  H
T  S  A  F  R  I  C  A  R
```

1 There are 15 words connected with the Roman games hidden in the word square opposite. Try to find them. You can read them in any direction.

2 Why were the games so important to the Romans?

3 Imagine you are a spectator at the games. Describe the sounds, sights and smells.

4 Draw up a day's programme for the games, and design a poster to advertise it to the citizens of Rome.

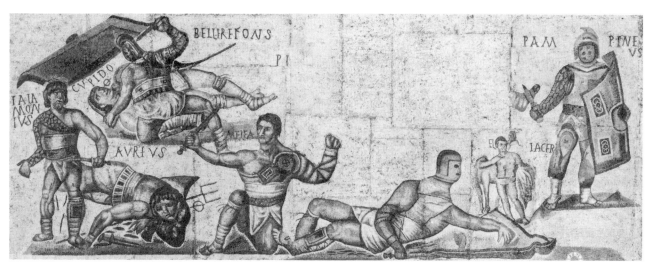

A mosaic showing gladiators fighting in the arena

Excavation at Giza

See Teachers' Notes page 5.

The questions below are for use in the detective exercise on pages 26 and 27. (For convenience, these questions may be duplicated for use within the school.)

Section A: *The excavation of the shaft*

1 What evidence is there that this was a secret burial? (facts **4** and **5**)

2 Why was the tomb so deep? (facts **12** and **13**)

3 What evidence is there that the tomb was not meant to be so deep? (facts **6, 7** and **11**)

4 Who probably built the tomb? (facts **9** and **10**)

Section B: *The discovery of the tomb*

1 What was the total time it took Dr Reisner to dig down the shaft and clear the tomb? (fact **15**)

2 Suggest why it took nearly a year to clear such a small tomb.

3 Using fact **16**, find 3 pieces of evidence to show the tomb was unfinished.

Section C: *The tomb*

1 What evidence is there from the funeral objects listed that the mummy was likely to be female?

2 Who was this likely to be?

3 What relation was this person to Cheops?

4 What evidence can you find from the shape of the shaft and the condition of the tomb that this burial was done in a hurry? (facts **8, 11** and **16**)

5 Explain Dr Reisner's 3 conclusions and how he reached them.

Section D: *The mystery*

Now write your report by copying and completing these sentences. Say how you came to your conclusions.

1 In the year 2070 BC, while King Cheops was supervising the building of his own mortuary temple at Giza, a messenger brought bad news from the Royal Cemetery at Dashur. The messenger said that . . .

2 However, Cheops was not told . . .
because . . .

3 Cheops then decided . . .

4 He gave his workmen clear orders . . .

5 But they faced a number of problems such as . . .

6 This meant that reburial was . . .

You may want to add some ideas of your own based on the evidence.

Section E: *Extra questions*

1 When and how did the alabaster chips get into the closed boxes?

2 Why was the sarcophagus reburied at Giza?

3 Why was the small pyramid near the entrance to the tomb not finished?

4 Why were the builders of the tomb in such a hurry?

5 Who smashed the canopy, and why?

6 Who was the most relieved in 2070 BC when the sarcophagus was reburied, and why?

64